D0846425

5-21-2008

TO TOM,

A DORCHESTER BRO
WHO HAS THE HISTORY TO
KNOW THE TRUTH WRITTEN
HERE, AND WHO DEFINITELY
KNOWS -- SPIRIT MATTERS!

WHERE HAVE ALL THE YEARS GONE?

PEACE,

MATT

SPIRIT
MATTERS

by

Matthew J. Pallamary

Mystic Ink Publishing

Mystic Ink Publishing
Carlsbad, CA
www.mysticinkpublishing.com
Phone: 1-800-839-8640

First published by Mystic Ink Publishing Februrary 14, 2008

© 2007 Matthew J. Pallamary. All Rights Reserved,

*No part of this book may be reproduced, stored in a retrieval system, or
transmitted by any means without the written permission of the author.*

ISBN: 978-1-4343-1801-5 (sc)
ISBN: 978-1-4343-1802-2 (hc)
Printed in the United States of America
Bloomington, Indiana

This book is printed on acid-free paper.

Library of Congress Control Number: 2007906066

Book Jacket and Page Design: Linda Gibbs/Malibu CA
Author's Photograph: Gibbs Photo/Malibu CA

BOOKS BY MATTHEW J. PALLAMARY

The Small Dark Room Of The Soul

Land Without Evil

Dreamland (With Ken Reeth)

A Short Walk To The Other Side

This book is dedicated to the loving memory of M.A.

It is returning, at last it is coming home to me—my own Self and those parts of it that have long been abroad and scattered among all things and accidents.

--Nietzsche
Thus Spoke Zarathustra

CONTENTS

I SEED

II SPROUT

III   BLOSSOM

I

SEED

PRELUDE

A Waking Dream

am outside of time and space, where the normal rules of perception no longer apply. Colors with hues that defy description bombard me, then unfold in multicolored geometric progressions that could be microcosmic quantum expressions or unfolding galaxies. Within these realms I have lived as an insect devoured by still bigger insects, which have in turn been devoured by lizards and snakes with long ethereal stomachs that have passed me into non-rational dimensions that both amaze and terrify.

Outside of my physical body, the frogs, birds, insects, jaguars, and other creatures of the Peruvian Amazon fill the night air with their calls, cries, twitters, and buzzes. For me there is no difference between the infinity expressing itself outside of me and the infinity that I soar through inside of me. It is all one. Outside of time and space, a noise from deep in the jungle sounds as if it is right beside me, startling me.

Sometimes I feel myself fully present and aware, in two places at the same time, often in different times and dimensions.

After experiencing the consciousness of predator and prey in the lower worlds, I have flown first as a condor, then as a hummingbird into sublime and exquisite high-frequency realities, exploding with neon luminescent pastel manifestations that defy rationality. While my spirit soars, my body quivers and my insides teeter on the verge of both vomiting and shitting.

I soar between agony and ecstasy as each experience awes my soul with a palette of emotions that range from heavenly bliss to a hellish, maddening terror that cannot be articulated, much less comprehended. I am vaguely aware of others sitting around me in the humid jungle night inside a circular open-air hut called a *maloca*. Many of them vomit and sometimes cry out in fear or bliss as they pass through their own visions. I feel my soul connected to theirs.

Our visions are directed by the music of a white-clad *mestizo* shaman who sings magical songs and plays different flutes and a stringed mandolin-like instrument called a charango. He is the keeper of a vast body of knowledge of Amazonian healing plants that dates back to prehistoric times. His specialty is a unique combination of plants that have brought me to this visionary state that continues to unfold outside of three-dimensional reality.

In this waking dream, where time and space become fluid, I not only soar through alien vistas of sight, sound, and feeling; I also travel through events of my life, both good and bad, often reliving them and their emotional content. Throughout my journey, I often confront hidden aspects of my self that have been ignored and denied because of the negative emotional charge that they hold. I sometimes vomit when confronted with something particularly unpleasant, which clears it out energetically in what is called a purge.

I have come a long way to this remote spot, deep in the primordial rain forest, far from civilization, to spend extended time isolated in nature to learn what the plants have to teach me, especially about myself. To be healed I must confront the forces that have driven and tortured me throughout my life so that I can understand the lessons that they have to teach me. To get to their root, I must travel back to my beginnings so I can come to terms with the energies that brought me into this life.

ONE

Domestic Bust

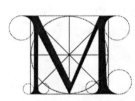y father Mickey embodied the archetype of the original party animal. It seemed like all he ever wanted to do was to have fun, regardless of the cost to himself or those around him, especially his family. His obsessive drive for a good time was his way of fleeing his demons of anger and frustration. I know this because I had his same maniacal drive, my "insane streak" that I inherited from my old man. Growing up and well into manhood, my insane streak often burst forth unexpectedly, raging from the shadows of my soul with deadly force, nearly killing me and damaging others with its explosive violence. When the impulse didn't arise from within, what lurked within was instinctively drawn to violence occurring outside of me, and when I didn't go to it, it came to me whether I liked it or not.

Along with my father's insane streak, I took on my mother's passive wound. Feeling unloved made me give, for acceptance from others, what I couldn't give myself. My female passive and male aggressive responses to feeling unloved acted like magnets, providing alternating polarities to the steady stream of violence that found its way to me.

My mother Colleen was born in Bridgeport, Connecticut in 1930, a middle child with an older brother and a younger sister. She went into show business at the age of three, when my tyrannical grandmother forced her into dancing and tumbling lessons after a doctor diagnosed her with rickets and ordered exercise. She worked hard practicing, but my grandmother, in her old-school thinking, equated harsh, unrelenting abuse with bringing out excellence. Every time my grandmother presided over my mother's practice, she made my mom nervous, causing her to falter. With each mistake, my grandmother picked her up by her feet and banged her head on the floor, literally driving the point home.

In those days of the Great Depression, there was no television, only radio. At age ten my mom competed in a nationwide talent contest on the Uncle Don Radio Show and took first place over thousands of other kids by reciting poetry while doing a hands-free headstand. Among other things, she won a trip to Hollywood, where she met Boris Karloff, Bella Lugosi, Jack Benny, Charlie Chan, and other well-known film actors of that time. My mother told me that the only reason she won was because the people running the contest wouldn't let my grandmother in to watch.

My mom's talents took her to New York City, where she worked in summer tours at the Roxy Theater, Radio City Music Hall, and numerous other venues. She graduated high school on a Friday afternoon and was on a train to New York Monday morning, on the road, working in a Vaudeville show. During the course of her career, she appeared on the Milton Berle show and worked with Frank Sinatra and many other up-and-coming acts of the pre-television era.

My father, born in Boston to a pair of World War I spies, served in the navy during World War II, stationed on the *USS California*, an aircraft carrier. He played the drums in the Navy Big Band until a kamikaze attack left him with shrapnel in his hip and his head, along with an addiction to codeine.

My parents met while touring with a traveling show in South America. Mickey worked as the show's drummer and my mom tumbled as an acrobat, part of a three-woman act. My old man romanced my mother with extravagant gestures like paying musicians to follow and serenade her, singing to her up on her balcony, constantly sending her flowers, and throwing money down to the poor people on the street to impress her.

When they played in Montevideo Uruguay, the show's producers left the country with all of the money, stranding everyone with no funds and no means of returning to the United States. It took a month for the federal government to repatriate my mother and fly her back to Connecticut. My father's family paid his way back to Boston immediately in the first of many efforts to separate my mother from their favorite son. When my mom returned home pregnant with my older sister, my paternal grandfather offered her a large sum of money to dissuade her from marrying my father, because the family didn't think a show girl was good enough for him.

Against the wishes of his parents, my father married my mother in Southbridge, Massachusetts in August of 1952. When they married, his mother checked in to Boston State Hospital for melancholia and psychotic depressive cachexia at age fifty-seven. She died there from pneumonia two years and twenty-seven days later, on my older sister's second birthday.

My mom decided to leave show business when my sister was born, feeling that the lifestyle and environment wouldn't be healthy for children. Little did she know that the environment she was entering would be even more chaotic than the instability of show business.

The mystery of my old man's parents and his mother's psychological breakdown, coupled with their hostility toward my mother, leaves me to wonder about the relationship between my father, the baby of his family, and his mother, whose mental health failed when he married. Whatever the enigma of their past held, my grandfather stayed in the spying business running a private-investigation agency in Boston, where Mickey worked as a private investigator while playing big band drums at night. My mom became a homemaker.

No one knew the whereabouts or activities of my shady grandfather at the time, but my father brought his psychotic mother home on weekends, where she often wandered around the house in the middle of the night until he awoke one night to find her standing over my infant sister's crib, clutching a big knife.

In the years preceding my birth, Mickey's antics had been painting an increasingly troubled picture. He always had crazy schemes to get someone else's money. Discrepancies became his opportunities, like the time he found out about a senator having an affair with a bartender's wife and tried blackmailing the senator. He often wheedled his way into then Senator Jack Kennedy's office or the office of Massachusetts Attorney General Bobby Kennedy, where he would steal notepads that said "From the desk of" and use them to write notes to people about himself to further his scams. One time he even stooped low enough to collect and pocket money for blinded veterans.

In his greed, my father teamed up with a professional safe cracker called a "peat man." In Irish lore, in which my mother was steeped, a peat man was a man who collected peat from the bogs to burn in the fireplace for heating. In slang terms, it describes a person who is tainted by a subconscious malevolence. Both of these definitions fit. To get into Boston's wealthy mansions, the peat man took all of his clothes off, greased himself down with lard, and slithered down the chimney. If he couldn't crack the safe there, he took it with him to crack somewhere else.

When the peat man hijacked a truckload of cigarettes, my father offered to stash them in our garage so the peat man could lay low and sell them off when the heat blew over. Following Mickey's advice, the man made himself scarce. As soon as he did, my old man sold the cigarettes and kept the money. Soon afterward my mom woke up in the middle of the night and found the big peat man sitting at the kitchen table. He wanted his money. His unexpected appearance scared the hell out of my mother. He had been to the house with my father before and my mom knew he liked tomato sandwiches, so she made him one and chided him for breaking in, telling him that my father wasn't there and to knock on the door like everyone else. She had a reputation for being honest, and everyone knew she had no involvement in Mickey's business, so the peat man respected her wishes. I don't think he ever caught up with my old man, but a few years later a gang caught up to

him in prison and beat him to death with baseball bats. Apparently his
subconscious malevolence caught up with him.

Mafia leg-breakers often came to the house looking for my old
man. They always respected my mom, but were intent on finding him.
More than once, he hid in the closet. My mother would say, "Go ahead
and look." They did, but lucky for Mickey, they didn't find him.

Some of his biggest trouble came from Boston cops running a
loan-sharking and bookmaking operation that went up the command
chain, all the way to the commissioner. When the pressure from them
grew too strong, Mickey went to the newspapers and ratted them out.
Of two people asked to testify in the ensuing investigation, one woman
fled in fear and ended up murdered.

My parents moved frequently around Boston because my old man
always failed to pay the rent. This also helped him stay one step ahead
of the leg-breakers or anybody else he ripped off. If it got really bad,
he dropped out of sight by checking himself in to the VA hospital. His
evasiveness made our lives increasingly chaotic until we moved into
a second-floor apartment, where my memories really begin. I had no
inkling that my parents teetered on the verge of divorce in my four-
year-old awareness. Mickey loved show business and playing the drums.
Going to clubs and watching him play made a strong impression on
me, and drumming became a big part of my life. My old man knew
Louie Bellson, Gene Krupa, and Buddy Rich: all famous big band
drummers. Aside from Mickey, my maternal grandfather used to sit in
his den most nights, playing on a practice pad to Dixieland jazz albums
with drumsticks that once belonged to Buddy Rich.

Playing the drums at night and working as a private investigator were
not your typical nine-to-five occupations. Mickey often disappeared
for days on end in a haze of pot, cigarettes, codeine, beer, liquor, and
god knows what else while he hustled, conned, and scammed his way
into innumerable schemes to get someone else's money.

With him mostly absent, my mother kept the nest. Auburn-haired,
with big blue eyes and an open, expressive face, my mom radiated love
to me like an open flower. I felt blessed to be the youngest of three
because it gave me the most time with her. With my older brother and
sister off to school, I had her all to myself. The voice of Frank Sinatra
singing "Love and Marriage" and other love songs often filled the

apartment while I played, feeling protected in my mother's presence. Some nights I awoke amid an invisible terror that sent me running to the safety of her bed, burrowing between her and my dad during the times he was there and sleeping contented beside her when he was not. In the mornings I loved sitting at the table with her for breakfasts of cinnamon sugar on toast with a splash of coffee and sugar in my milk. Throughout all of my old man's madness, my mother never said anything bad about him, and for the most part she protected and insulated us from the brunt of his insanity. Home life with my mom felt warm, safe, and loving.

I remember one Christmas Eve when we had no presents and no tree. Later that night we heard noise from the front hall followed by my old man lumbering up the stairs with a tree, presents, and everything else, giving us a last-minute, instant Christmas, and a good one; the last one I ever had with him. I also remember being in the apartment one cold winter day with my mom while my brother and sister attended school. Our heat and electricity had been turned off because the bill hadn't been paid, and my old man's father had taken the tires off of our car as part of his perpetual vendetta against my mom. I was chilly, huddled under her winter jacket eating a jelly sandwich, the only food left in the house. A friend of my mom's came and took us in for a couple of weeks until my old man showed up to take us home again.

My parents' marriage deteriorated to the point of erupting violence that I unwittingly played out in microcosm as a victim at the age of four. I had my back to the kid across the street one day when a sharp stab shot through the back of my head. I screamed in pain and turned to see the kid's face twisted in anger, a broken pencil clutched in his hand. He stabbed me so hard the point had broken off. The shock of seeing this drove my anguished wails harder because I had no idea why he had attacked me. My first cries came from my physical pain but were soon eclipsed by a deeper, more troubling emotional wound that raised a horrifying question. How could an unprovoked person inflict such dark and violent anger on another?

In spite of my mom's love, this incident became my reluctant introduction into warrior training on the street and one of many instances that fueled my own rage and illusion of being unlovable. At the same time that I suffered at the hands of this enraged kid, the main event unfolded between my parents, heralded by my old man's increasingly erratic behavior. Lately he had been home, sitting at his desk in an office at the front of the house, terrifying my mother by pointing his unloaded gun at her, pulling the trigger over and over again. Soon afterward he lost his cool and exploded.

I remember watching from the bedroom closet, where I hid behind a shoe rack. I had a clear view of my father in the dining room, smashing all of my mother's treasured Frank Sinatra records, then loading his gun and waving it around, muttering and swearing. Everyone else had run from the apartment, but I stayed hidden. In his rage my father went out to the back porch, picked up a metal crib over his head, and hurled it down at my mother and sister from the second floor porch.

I slipped out when the house grew quiet and some neighbors took me in while the cops surrounded the house, filling the afternoon with flashing blue lights and a cop's voice booming through a megaphone, "Come out with your hands up."

I never saw my old man in the house after that, and my parents separated soon afterward. With three kids to raise by herself and a fourth on the way, my mom moved us to Dorchester, a tough blue-collar Irish-Catholic ghetto in Boston, where we could start our lives over again without my old man.

TWO

Burning Down the House

 have a yellowed cartoon cut out from *The Dorchester Reporter* entitled "The Power of Perception," by an artist named Gus D'Angelo that characterizes Dorchester well. It shows a clean-cut guy in a suit and tie extending his hand in greeting, saying, "Hi! I'm from Dorchester." Beside him a wide-eyed guy with his hair standing on end has dropped his paper and has his hands in the air, yelling, "Don't shoot! Don't shoot!"

In 1960, before I turned six, we moved into a five-room apartment on the second and third floors of a big green house in Dorchester. Soon after moving, my mother gave birth to my younger sister. Shortly after that she had a surprise visit from two cops who came to question her. My father had tipped them off that she took bets and ran a bookmaking operation out of the house. Seeing my newborn little sister and my mother's demeanor, the cops quickly saw through my father's lie.

In less than a year, we moved two houses up the street to number seven, the first house on the block at the top of a small hill. There we settled into a first-floor five-room flat in a traditional Dorchester three-decker wooden-frame house sided with cracked and broken gray slate siding and topped with a gabled slate roof. Dorchester has miles of these three-decker apartment houses running up and down street after street. My mother worked hard, with an artistic flair, painting, wallpapering, and doing whatever else she could to create a nice home for us. She made a work of art out of the apartment's ancient raised bathtub when she painted it gold with a huge, elegant red rose on its side. She knew how to sew too, making everything from clothes to curtains.

The outside world looked quite different from our cozy nest because we lived in the first house at the top of a hill. Our side and tiny back yards bordered the back lots of an L-shaped line of connected storefronts that ran along two main streets that intersected with other commercial blocks, making up an area known as Four Corners.

Across the street from our house stood a Texaco station. Looking at the front of our house from the gas station, you could see a line of houses going down the hill to the left. In the narrow passage to the right of our house, the dry cleaners vented their steam pipes every Monday through Saturday morning at six.

Down the alley, past the dry cleaners on our right, ran a line of connected storefronts enclosed in a long red brick building. Past the dry cleaners, a Chinese laundry bordered with a broken-down wooden fence hid the dreaded Chinese dog, a hairy beast that bit me thirteen times. One time he chased me to the top of a fire escape before sinking his teeth into my calf. We never knew if he would be out and could never see him lurking behind the fence because of his mottled brown fur, but when he attacked, he lunged through the broken fence with demonic fury.

Beside the Chinese laundry, the sound of clicking billiards came all hours of the day and night from a pool hall that I was never old enough to go into. Next in line came a Laundromat, and on the end of the block on the corner beside our back yard stood a drugstore that connected the line of businesses beside our house with another line that ran the length of the block along the back yards of all the houses on our street.

A delicatessen with a second-floor apartment above it, directly behind our house, joined the drugstore on the corner. Beside it, going down the block in order, were a meat market/liquor store, a five-and-dime, a real estate office, a dentist's office with apartments above it, and on the far end, a Christian Science Reading Room.

In a short period of time, I knew every rooftop and billboard, all the trees, fire escapes, and drainpipes that led up and down from the roof. I loved to climb everything, especially trees. I often climbed high into them until their branches barely held me, then swayed in the breeze, looking down at the ground, driving myself to the edge of panic, imagining what it would be like to fall. When I reached the point of shivering terror, I pulled it back in and calmed myself, loosening my white-knuckled grip until I reached equilibrium.

Once there, I did it again, taking myself back to the edge of terror, where I pushed past the previous point before pulling back again, repeating the cycle. I did this over and over, going from trees to rooftops, to third-floor porches, later graduating to towers, bridges, cliffs, and other precipices. I felt compelled to explore my fear and its dynamics. Sometimes the urge to jump arose, and I explored that too, but I only pushed past that one when I had water below to break my fall. My fear of heights and the swiftness of its onset fascinated me, making its boundaries something I felt driven to test again and again.

Our house had the smallest back yard of all. The deli behind us had a bigger yard surrounded by a wooden fence. The meat market/liquor store and the five-and-dime in the middle of the block had no fences, making an open space behind the two houses beside us, giving the neighborhood kids a big lot to play in. We usually played what we called squash, which had the same rules as baseball, except you punched a soccer-ball-sized ball and ran the bases. If someone on the defending team caught the ball or hit you with it while you were running, you were out.

Out in the street in front of our house, we played stickball or half-ball using a broomstick for a bat to hit a cut-in-half pimple ball, which was a white hollow baseball-sized ball covered with small, raised stars that had been punctured. It took a special skill to make the halves sail like Frisbees and even more skill to hit such a small, fast-flying, hollow half-ball with something as thin as a broomstick. If we had an inflated ball or another small rubber ball that actually bounced, we played three-flies-out by throwing it against the front steps of a house, trying to bounce it over the defender's head.

I started first grade in this neighborhood and soon learned that being a small kid made me an easy target for bullies. I experienced my second reluctant warrior's initiation when two bigger kids took turns beating me over the head with their metal lunchboxes. Once more I bore the physical pain, followed by a deeper, more troubling emotional wound that begged the question of how people could inflict such violence in an unprovoked attack.

The last memorable time I had fun with my father, he took me, my older brother, and big sister to Nantasket Beach, an amusement park on Boston's South Shore where my godfather, Hot Ticket, worked a game booth. I always thought my godfather's name came from the fact that he gave us free tickets to the rides, especially this night, when we rode them long after closing. I found out years later that he worked as a private investigator for my grandfather and took bets as a bookie for the mob. His game booth gave him a perfect front for his operation. We had the time of our lives staying out late that night with my father. My mother was nervous and upset when he finally brought us home. We didn't know that the cops had left moments before. My father was supposed to have us home by six o'clock, but he had kept us out until midnight after telling my mother that he would drive us off a bridge if she called the cops on him.

He often waited for me in his car on the way home from school. If I went to the store for my mother, he would be parked halfway around the block, sometimes with a friend. He always asked questions about my mom, but I never had anything to say except "Where's my allowance?"

I didn't know that he never paid child support to my mother. He had been busy taking ten thousand dollars from some Chinese people, promising to get their relatives into the country. In typical style, he kept their money and didn't deliver on his promise. Now the cops were closing in on him. I think this is what pushed him over the edge when he flipped out.

My mother had him in court for non-support until the cops asked her to stop the court action so they could prosecute him for embezzling from the Chinese people. She did as they asked; opening the door for them to send him to Walpole State Prison for three years, home of luminaries like the Boston Strangler. With no income or means of support, we had to go on welfare.

With a warrant out for his arrest, he came around the neighborhood trying to get to us kids, but my mother spotted him and pointed him out to the cops, who came and arrested him. Shortly after his arrest, a neighbor knocked on the door one morning and asked my mother if the women's underwear strewn across the front hedges belonged to her. To her horror, they had been taken from the clothesline on the back porch and put on display in the front of the house. Not long after that, we awoke in the middle of the night to the sound of a neighbor pounding on the back door, yelling, "Fire!"

Flames engulfed the back porch, spreading to the porch above and the back of the house. Our neighbor threw buckets of water on the fire while my mother called the fire department. Within minutes, firemen and hoses ran down the hall and through the kitchen, where our dog Tippy stayed curled up under the kitchen table. The firemen hustled us out of the house in our pajamas onto the front porch, where we waited for them to put the fire out.

In the seven years that we lived in the first-floor apartment at number seven, three cars went up in flames in front of our house. One of them became fully engulfed in a blazing inferno. To this day I don't know how the gas tank didn't blow. We never knew who set the cars on fire because things like that happened in Dorchester, although ours seemed to be the only house on our street that it happened to. Though I will never know who torched the cars, I do know that my father was the one who lit the house on fire with us inside.

THREE

License To Steal

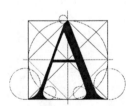t some point in my childhood, I heard that Boston had one rat for every person that lived there. We heard stories of rats falling through the ceilings and landing in baby's cribs to chew away at their helpless little faces in the Franklin Field projects in Dorchester, or the D Street projects in South Boston. I never saw any in our apartment, but I lived in constant fear of them after someone told me that if you cornered one it would jump for your throat. This image made me walk the side alley and darkened hall outside our back door in a state of hyper-vigilance. I saw lots of nasty gray, feral rats literally as big as cats, running along the subway tracks and gutters. A friend and I killed one with bricks and big rocks when we saw it running along the gutter in front of our house. Once while fishing with a drop line off of a pier in Dorchester bay, I saw a huge rat on the rocks below, eating from the side of a big, dead fish. When I threw rocks at

it, it stopped and glared defiantly up at me without running. Its feral rodent intelligence spooked me.

I had my worst experience when a rat scrambled out of a neighbor's cellar. I watched in fascination as a man trapped it in a corner with the tine of a pitchfork. The rat let out an ungodly, bone chilling squeal when the pitchfork tine pierced its neck. Its death shriek sent the huge dog that lived there bounding over the fence, onto my back, where he sank his teeth into my shoulder, ripping skin and drawing blood before I escaped. My mother insisted on rushing me to the hospital herself, so the cops gave us a flashing-light cop-car escort. Though bruised and bloody from the bite, my shoulder had no serious damage, but everyone feared rabies, so I had to get a Tetanus shot, which I thought was for rabies.

My father possessed many of the same qualities as Boston's rodents. He stole from the blind, ripped off the Chinese immigrants, and he had the balls to steal from the Mafia. He always had someone looking for him, which explained his evasive rat-like behaviors. Before he went to prison, where they killed people for being rats, my mother finagled her marginal resources, probably with the help of my grandmother, and got bicycles for me, my brother, and my older sister. We kept them under our back porch until someone stole them a few weeks later. I found out years later that it was my father who had stolen from me! The theft of my bicycle became a foundation for my rage, causing me to rationalize stealing as a fact of life. In Dorchester I discovered the truth of this over and over again.

By dropping fifteen cents into a milkshake cup at the front door, we could go to the YMCA on the next block and spend all day playing basketball, wrestling, or candlepin bowling on four lanes downstairs, where we had to set our pins by hand. On Fridays they had record hops for younger kids and dances with live bands for the teenagers.

I walked out onto our back porch one day and saw a dark-haired older guy that I recognized down in our back yard emptying the change from the Y's cup. Obie, who must have been in his late teens then, would become my main connection for buying alcohol in the years to come. Nobody knew where he lived, where he came from, or his age, but he remained a regular fixture in Dorchester from as far back as I can remember.

Obie looked up and saw that I recognized the cup. Without missing a beat, he handed me thirty-five cents and said, "Keep your mouth shut."

I did.

This transaction initiated me into what we called "Dorchester rules." In this case the unwritten rule said, "Keep your mouth shut and never rat off anyone." Soon afterward I started pilfering money from my mother's pockets and purse. I never took any bills; only loose change, and only if I thought she wouldn't miss it.

One Sunday morning I discovered that the front door of a newly opened record store across the street had been left unlocked. I went in, closed the door behind me, and helped myself to stacks of forty-five records. With the "license to steal" that my father gave me, I stole from stores often; sometimes because I wanted something, other times just for the thrill. I learned how to switch price tags and once or twice walked straight out the front door of a store with a big item in my arms as if I owned the place. My only bust came when my mother caught me with things I stole from a variety store. She brought me back, made me confess, and return the merchandise.

Early in my teenage years, my friends and I stole stingray bikes with sissy bars, banana seats, and ape-hanger handlebars. After dismantling them we repainted the frames and swapped the parts around. My bicycle made of stolen parts was stolen from me three times. I stole it back twice.

Through all of my thievery, I had my own distorted moral code. Aside from the change pilfered from my mother, I never stole from anyone that I knew, and I never took anything from a home where I was a guest. I saw this as disrespectful and a violation of another unwritten Dorchester rule: "never rip off your friends."

The famous South Boston Brinks armored car robbery of the 50s, glorified in the movie with Peter Falk, held legendary status in Dorchester and Southie. No one ever caught the thieves, which made them admired and looked upon as heroes because they had outsmarted the system. To further bolster my license to steal, during my impressionable childhood, a popular television show called *It Takes a Thief*, starring Robert Wagner, aired weekly, portraying thieving and burglary as cool, sophisticated, and glamorous. This open glorification had a big impact on forming one of my primary ambitions in life, a desire to be a successful career criminal.

I thought I could outdo my father, whom I last saw when I was seven, before he went to prison. I only saw him two more times in my life, once when I was fourteen at his father's funeral and once when I was twenty-one, home on leave from the air force. He died of amyotrophic lateral sclerosis, otherwise known as Lou Gehrig's disease, before I turned twenty-seven. I lived in California at the time and didn't go back for his funeral.

FOUR

Warrior Training

Before serial killers became so prevalent in our culture, I lived in the shadow of the Boston Strangler, one of the most infamous killers of the twentieth century. The strangler visited Boston neighborhoods posing as plumbers, electricians, or other repairmen that trusting females let into their homes. Once inside, he brutally raped and strangled them.

The specter of the strangler occupied much of my imagination. In my mind no one was safe, especially my single mother, whom I thought of as a prime target. I dreaded being outside when night came and darkness crept in. My brother, older sister, and I huddled close in terror soon after nightfall, half expecting the strangler to leap out at us when we walked home my sister's friend, who lived two houses away.

Fear followed me into my dreams, and I often awoke in fright to sinister noises like the sound of a tree branch scratching the window.

These fears became reality one hot summer night when I awoke to my mother's hoarse quavering voice on the phone telling the cops, "I just startled a man climbing in our back window." The alarming terror I heard dancing beneath her words amplified my own.

She had been sitting up late watching television when a sudden intuition reminded her that she had left the back kitchen window open. When she started down the hall, she looked out a side window and spotted a man taking his shoes off and tiptoeing down the alley between our house and the cleaners. Keeping in the shadows of the hallway, she watched in horror as he climbed up over the back porch railing and started into our apartment through the back window. Not wanting to frighten us, my mother took a deep breath, and in a low voice said, "Screw!"

I often wonder what would have happened if my mother hadn't followed her intuition that night.

Daylight brought its own challenges. By the age of nine, I grew tired of getting picked on. I never wanted to fight back, but being small meant that the bullying never stopped, so I had to learn how to defend myself. A blond, blue-eyed, freckle-faced kid named Paul lived in the corner house of the next block down the street. He was the fourth in a family of five brothers. His father was a typical Irish Boston cop. I hung around with all of them except the youngest, but I connected more with Paul than the others. He and I used to watch the big kids hide their beer and steal it after the cops chased them off. I drank my first beer with Paul at the age of seven and started smoking cigarettes around the same time. The big kids taught me how to inhale, which made me cool.

Paul and I fought a lot, egged on by the bigger kids. We took pride in the fact that we bloodied each other's noses, knocked each other's teeth out, and gave each other black eyes—and we stayed friends. Paul had lots of practice fighting with his brothers and won our first few fights until I figured out that he won by whacking me with the same haymaker from somewhere near ground level. Once I figured that out, I saw it coming and blocked it, followed by a haymaker of my own that took him out.

Each time we fought, the bigger kids formed a circle around us, betting on who would win, and whoever won got a piece of the action, usually somewhere around thirty-five cents. One day while Paul and I battled it seemed like the only people in the world consisted of him and me in the ring until I flew into the air. I looked up, shocked to see my mother holding me by the collar. She bawled everyone out, ending my days of paid battles with Paul.

One day when Paul and I went around the corner by the dry cleaners, a big, fat black kid confronted us, putting the tip of a pocket knife blade against my stomach. He pushed on it, saying, "Give me all your money."

I had fifteen cents, but I wasn't going to give it up.

He took us further around the corner and continued. "Give me all your money or I'm going to stab you."

"I swear, I don't have any," I said, holding my palms out.

After an interminable time in our stand off, he put the knife back in his pocket and walked away. When he had gone halfway down the block, I yelled out, "Except for the two bucks in my shoe, nigger!"

He turned and barreled toward me like an enraged rhino. Paul and I ducked around the corner, running into a gang of our friends who had shown up in front of my house. When the black kid came around the corner after us, I yelled to my friends, "The nigger tried to take my money. Get him!"

We ran after him, but he had a good head start, so we let him get away. This confrontation preceded the bussing and race riots Boston and other big cities had in the 60s, when the blacks moved into our neighborhood. The first time a black family moved into the second-floor apartment next door, they threw their garbage out the window into the alley. This and the knife didn't give me a good impression of black people. Since then I've lost track of how many times I had knives pulled on me, but black kids always did it, and they always outnumbered us and stood taller than me.

Paul stayed one of my best friends until his family moved from Dorchester to Quincy. I visited him once after that. A few years later, two guys got into a scuffle over a drug deal at a playground near his house. Paul stepped in to break it up and one of the guys stabbed him in the throat, killing him. Since his death I have had more than one nightmare about being Paul on the receiving end of the blade.

FIVE

The *Real* Hand of God

oth Dorchester and South Boston had large Irish-Catholic neighborhoods. Each parish covered two or three square miles, making Catholic churches, rectories, and schools the dominating feature of many city blocks. Funeral homes dotted every few blocks and bars peppered many corners, somehow balancing out the influence of the church, while keeping an ancient Irish connection alive between drinking, dying, and God. My grandmother was a hardcore Catholic, so the church made a big impression on my feelings about God and religion.

I never liked going to church, except in my younger years when we visited my grandmother in Connecticut. I loved getting up at first light with my grandfather and going to early mass with him. Aside from the quiet sunrise drive down rural roads, spotting deer and other early morning wildlife, we made it home before everyone else woke up. I was

24

thrilled with the notion that they had to get ready for church while I got to put on my play clothes and do whatever I wanted.

I distinctly remember sitting in church around the age of six, listening to the sermons, disbelieving most of what they told me. Sitting, kneeling, standing, and praying through monotone invocations, half of which were unintelligible Latin, felt like hypnotic, mind-numbing calisthenics. I felt no sense of the divine in any of it.

It felt more like dog obedience training.

Mortal sins, venial sins, confessions, and ritual—not to mention what would happen if you transgressed—soured me on all of it. I couldn't believe that being Catholic made me "saved," while people who worshipped in other ways would not be saved. If God planned on sending me to heaven for being a good Catholic, why couldn't he do the same for Protestants, Indians, Jews, Buddhists, pagans, or the myriad of other believers? How could God damn them if they didn't know or hadn't accepted Jesus? If God thought that way, I didn't want to be in his heaven. I'd rather be in hell with everybody else.

What the church said didn't ring true, and the things I saw "devout" Catholics doing the other six days of the week drove the point home. My mom went to church a few times in my early childhood, but I knew her heart wasn't in it, and as soon as we grew old enough, we went by ourselves. My brother and I soon learned to keep our money, instead of putting it into the collection basket, so we could go to the bakery after church and gorge ourselves on warm, mouthwatering honey-dipped doughnuts for six cents apiece. At first we went to church followed by Sunday school. Then we skipped Sunday school. After that we dropped church and Sunday school altogether.

Paul must not have been old enough, but my brother and I usually met his older brothers, Tommy and Bobby, every Sunday morning. Together we had a lot more fun than sitting, kneeling, and genuflecting. We often went to a big park near the church, where we found dozens of beer, booze, and wine bottles from all the drinking that had gone on the night before. After smashing them on the sidewalk, we rang the citizen's alarm and hid to watch the cops rush in to find nothing.

We found a small construction storage yard in one of the neighborhoods with garages surrounding it on three sides. After climbing a ten-foot chain-link gate, we discovered stacks of mats piled in the space between the garages. We spent many Sunday mornings having the time of our lives jumping off the garage roofs into the pile of mats below until one morning I heard a lady yell at me, "Get off that roof before you hurt yourself!"

I knew she couldn't see the mats from her second-story window, so I yelled back, "I can't take it anymore. I want to kill myself!" Then I jumped. She screamed and we ran for the gates, barely making it over the fence when the cops came flying down the street. We scattered in terror, narrowly escaping a bust.

I only went to Sunday school once or twice in the eighth grade and knew hardly anything about Catholicism, yet I somehow managed to make my confirmation, satisfying the fears of those around me and appearing right in the eyes of the hierarchy I had been born into, but I never gave my heart to it. With all the pedophile scandals that came to light in the Catholic church, I feel as if I was blessed to be guided and protected from those and other dangers I had to deal with back then.

The age of nine became a rite of passage for me. Aside from having my first knife pulled on me, death became a reality with the loss of a friend, my mom's uncle, and something I witnessed firsthand. The Grim Reaper appeared frequently in the years to come, taking many friends; some violently, like Paul, others in tragic accidents. I witnessed so much death in those earlier years that for most of my life I had an aversion to the smell of flowers, whose cloying scents I associated with the essence of death.

Our friends Jimmy and his younger brother Jackie hung around with me, my brother, and my older sister. One day Jimmy, who was around twelve, went swimming at Houghton's Pond in the Blue Hills, south of Boston where he entangled his legs in weeds and drowned. It felt surreal seeing him lifeless in a coffin at a funeral home. It looked like Jimmy, but not the Jimmy I knew. He looked bloated and grotesque under all the thick makeup they had put on him. I saw death up close and personal soon afterward.

We lived a couple of miles from Dorchester bay in Boston Harbor and often swam there. Boston's Malibu Beach ran around a small bay that connected it to Savin Hill Beach and the Dorchester yacht club. A big cement bridge with a metal drawbridge separated the bay from the ocean. We loved jumping off the bridges into the channel, sometimes waiting for the lifeguards to chase us. We let them get within inches from grabbing us before jumping. When we felt extra bold and wanted a bigger thrill, we climbed up under the girders of the drawbridge and hung on while it rose, jumping or diving into the channel from the higher position of the raised drawbridge after the boat passed underneath.

Narrow wooden piers extended from both sides of the drawbridge out into the water with lights on the end so boats could see the channel in the dark. These piers also carried electrical power to the bridge. When the lifeguards chased us off the bridge, we jumped off of the piers instead.

This same summer, as I was waiting to climb the pier, I heard someone scream the moment the bridge went up. Looking up, I saw a teenager laying on his back on top of the pier, arched backward, his mouth wide in agonized screams. Wet from swimming, he had stretched out across the cable that carried power to the bridge. They couldn't put the bridge down because they didn't want to send more current through him. This caused a traffic jam that added to the spectacle until two lifeguards lifted him off the cable using towels under his neck and legs.

A burn the width and depth of the cable had been seared into the smoking flesh, muscle, and bone of his lower back. They strapped him to a stretcher board and rushed him away in an ambulance, but he died a few hours later. This time I had witnessed death's calling with my own eyes. It's charred, smoking image is forever imprinted in my memory.

SIX

Continuing Education

iving on welfare, my mother kept us clothed, fed, and sheltered. On hot, unbearable summer days, I spent my mornings hunting for bottles, getting two cents for smaller ones and nickels for bigger ones. If I collected eighteen cents or so, I asked my mother for the difference so I could reach my goal of twenty-five cents for car fare to Boston's Metropolitan District Commission pool in Hyde Park, the suburb where I thought the people with money lived. For ten cents I rode a bus, a trolley, and another bus that took me out of Dorchester. A nickel got me into the pool, and the last dime got me home.

When it snowed and school cancellations were announced over the radio, my brother and I hit the streets with our shovels, shoveling out cars, sidewalks, and driveways. In the warmer weather I worked as a bag boy at the local supermarket, packing groceries, and bringing them home in my wagon for tips. As I grew older, I understood that making money meant you had to hustle and that some hustles paid off better than others. On Sundays, if we wanted to go to the movies, we put a quarter in the newspaper machine, took out all the newspapers, and rode the subways selling them. When the Fourth of July came, we bought illegal firecrackers for eight dollars a bundle, giving us eighty packs that we sold for twenty-five cents each, making a twelve-dollar profit for every bundle we moved. When the Pop Warner football league did their fund drive after school started, we fished the collection cans out of the dumpster at the Y and went out on our own collections.

A church stood on the corner of the next block down the street from our house, followed by the Y, a funeral home, and a park called Mother's Rest. My brother and our friends attended the Boy Scouts at the church, played at the Y, and hung out at Mother's Rest, where I smoked my first cigarettes and drank my first beer. Mother's Rest had a good-sized hill with park benches that offered a view of Dorchester Bay, bordered by Washington Street at the top and our street at the bottom. We played baseball at the bottom of the hill during summers and had great rides down the hill in the winter using sleds, toboggans, cardboard boxes, ironing boards, refrigerator doors, and anything else that looked like it might slide.

As more blacks moved in, Washington Street became a border between the black and white neighborhoods. The first time black kids came to "our park" to sled, we chased them out. They dropped a sled in their flight, so we grabbed it, smashed it into pieces, and hung it from a big tree halfway up the hill with a sign that said "This is what happens to niggers who come to our park."

The feelings went both ways. During this time, two big black kids confronted me, threatening to knife me if I didn't give them my money. I reached into my back pocket like a cowboy ready to draw, threatening to stab the first one who wanted to try to take my money. They backed off and left me alone. I didn't have a knife.

I did well in my first years of grammar school, often making the honor roll or honorable mention. In the fourth grade, I became one of the first kids to learn new math, which I showed to the PTA. It got me in the newspaper. I won the school spelling bee in the sixth grade and competed in an inter-city match, coming within one person of winning a fifty-dollar savings bond, losing on one of the I-before-

E exceptions. I also passed the test to get into Boston Latin, the top school in the city that went from seventh to twelfth grade. Geared toward producing doctors and lawyers for Harvard, Latin only took the best and the brightest.

After starting the seventh grade, it soon became clear that I could not make it in Boston Latin. Because it was located in the Back Bay section of Boston, far from Dorchester, I had to take two buses and a train, passing through Dudley Street station in the middle of Roxbury, the all-black section of Boston. Every class at Latin gave a huge homework load, many with more than one book. Aside from being short with too many books to carry through one of the worst parts of Boston, I couldn't keep up with the workload. It gave me no time to play, and at the age of twelve I had no desire to be studying all the time. My grades plummeted, so I left Latin and transferred to Oliver Wendell Holmes, a mostly black junior high on the other side of Washington Street from Mother's Rest. At the "Ollie" my white skin stood out and I experienced prejudice firsthand because of the color of my skin.

On the day Martin Luther King was assassinated, they dismissed us early from school and I found myself thrust into an angry crowd of blacks, many of them much older than me. I felt the hostility in the air as one of a white minority. The looks felt bad enough, then came the angry words.

"Honky."

"Cracker."

"White trash."

Finally someone swung a board at me and I broke into a run along with a few other white kids. We retreated, throwing rocks and bottles at our pursuers while our fear propelled us faster than any of them could run.

I told my mom what had happened and told her that I refused to go back to the Ollie. She called the school board and a few days later they transferred me to Woodrow Wilson Junior High, a mostly white school. Though further to get to, the "Woodie" felt bigger, safer, and better.

SEVEN

Bully for You

ater in life I heard a man on the radio by the name of Roy Masters say, "You will become what you hate." It sounded odd and contradictory at first, but the more I considered it, the more I realized its truth. I hated having my bike stolen, so I became a thief. The same thing happened with bullying.

In the fourth grade, I got jumped by a kid named Arnie, who had been held back three times between stays at the Youth Service Board, Boston's main juvenile detention center, where many of my friends ended up. I never bothered him and he didn't scare me, but I left school late one day and found him waiting for me with another big goon. Without me seeing it, his friend got down on his hands and knees behind me and Arnie pushed me, sending me flying to the ground. My mom appeared as if out of nowhere, surprising all of us when she pulled up and yelled at big, stupid Arnie and his friend for being bullies. Her intuition had come through again, like it had with my fights with Paul, and the guy climbing in the back window. Arnie went back to jail a few weeks later, never to trouble me again.

When I had enough of getting picked on, having gained the confidence to take care of myself in a fight, I became a bully myself. It all started in the sixth grade with a kid named Jackie who I wanted to fight because I knew that I scared him. I chased him all the way home, empowered by the cheers of a good-sized audience. My second experience in the realm of bullying came at the urging of a black kid whose friendship made a lasting mark on me. After my transfer from the mostly black Ollie to the mostly white Woodie, I saw hardly any black kids, but we had one in our eighth-grade class named Bruce. Some of the kids at the Woodie feared him, but he treated me with respect, so I liked him. I'm sure part of it had to do with the fact that I had spent more time around black kids than the others, but beneath it all, the greater truth is that we simply connected as friends. I had only known Bruce a short time when, waiting for the bus one morning, he asked me to go with him to talk to another kid, saying, "All you have to do is stand there. I'll do the talking."

Intrigued, I followed him and stood quietly beside him while he demanded the other kid's lunch money. After the kid gave it up, Bruce split it with me. I only had to stand there and cross my arms for effect. On one of my last days in the eighth grade, Bruce and I missed the bus and had to walk home after staying late to let the air out of our math teacher's tires. Two younger black kids who hung around with Bruce joined us, and together we went into a variety store and grabbed a six-pack of sodas, candy, chips, and other stuff. We approached the counter, then ran out the door with everything we could carry.

The enraged storekeeper came bolting after us. Sodas fell out of the six-pack, shattering on the sidewalk. We dropped other items but escaped with most of our loot. When we divided our spoils in the aftermath, we had three bottles of soda for four of us. Bruce's friend took the last one, saying, "The white boy shouldn't have it."

Bruce grabbed the soda from his friend and gave it back to me, berating the other kid, saying, "My friendship with him doesn't have anything to do with color." The younger kid respected me after that. Bruce had shown us what partners and real friends meant. His actions made a big impression on me. Loyalty meant something to him, regardless of color or anyone else's opinion.

What a gift.

Getting transferred to the Woodie had other good points. My fighting friend Paul's older brother Bobby went there along with some of the other kids from my neighborhood. Going to school with them felt like an extension of our former church and Sunday school adventures. It didn't take long before the idea to skip arose, giving me my first thrills of playing hooky from public school. Once I had a taste of how much fun hooking school could be, it hooked me.

Sometime in my mid-teens, I realized that fear and cowardice made bullies, and with that revelation, something clicked, and I became protector to the underdog. After years of being the target, I stepped in to fight back. Even if I lost, I prided myself on fighting hard and I always gained respect. If I found myself in danger of being overpowered, I could grab a rock, board, or bottle to use as an equalizer. My mother could only protect me for so long. Soon I would be protecting her and my sisters, not only on the streets but in our own home.

During this time my mother met Jim, a divorced truck driver with three kids of his own. Tall, dark-haired, and heavyset, he lived with us in our first-floor apartment for a couple of years before we all moved into an old, rundown mansion a few houses down the street from the Dorchester courthouse, where I saw many of my friends sent to jail. Our downstairs had three rooms, a big kitchen, living room, and four fireplaces. The second floor had been split into a separate six-room apartment, leaving two separate rooms upstairs for my brother and I after fourteen years of sharing one.

My mom married big Jim and he found out how protective I was of her when he came home drunk one night. I awakened to the sound of their voices and heard pain in my mother's quavering voice following the sound of him hitting her. He didn't beat her, but in his drunkenness he played too rough and he wouldn't stop. Angry and frightened, I grabbed a baseball bat, went downstairs, and confronted him, saying, "If you lay one more hand on her, I'll beat your brains in, and if you ever lay a hand on her ever again, I'll beat your fucking brains in."

He stopped and fell silent while my mother held me back. After that he respected me and went out of his way to do nice things for me, and as far as I know, he never raised a hand to my mother after that.

We both knew I meant what I said.

EIGHT

Hot Boxes

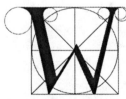ith my old man in prison and big Jim in the
picture, my mom felt safe for the first time
in years. She went to night school to learn
bookkeeping and when my little sister grew big
enough, my mom went to work. We moved from
the apartment to the mansion before I turned fourteen, at a time when
Boston seethed with racism and escalating violence. I didn't think my
brother felt the same protectiveness as I did, so I had to get tougher so
I could watch out for my mom and sisters.

My mom had a blast redecorating the inside of the crumbling
turn-of-the-century mansion, which felt like a castle compared to
the apartment we had lived in. She brightened the ancient carved
decorative kitchen woodwork with pink enamel and papered, painted,
and adorned the rest of our part of the mansion, making it home. Best

of all, after almost fourteen years, for the first time in my life I had my own room!

A street the next block over from ours had concrete steps at the top of a hill that became our hangout. The Alpha Road gang my brother and I became part of had some of our friends from Boy Scouts, some from Mother's Rest, and other kids from different streets. Only a few of the kids who hung out there actually lived on Alpha Road. As our gang grew, so did my friendships with Joey, Dell, and Mickey, all blossoming car thieves who spent their time bouncing in and out of jail.

I first met baby-faced Dell when we were thirteen. He and his two older brothers all had straight blond hair, round freckled faces, and big lower lips that stuck out like they were pouting. I couldn't believe how confidently Dell drove when he picked me up in his father's car. Scared shitless, I looked everywhere for the cops. Luckily we only drove a few blocks, but those first few joyrides paved the way for Dell's career.

Joey had his own flair and style. The youngest of three brothers, both he and his brother Frankie hung around with us. Both had short curly hair and sleepy blue eyes that disguised quick minds. Joey started stealing cars young, just like Dell.

Mickey and I met through his cousin Johnny and we spent time in the Boy Scouts together, but the Boy Scouts didn't make much of an impression on Mickey. Short and heavyset with wild curly brown hair and wild blue eyes that barely contained his rage, Mickey would fly into a rage at the slightest provocation. We fought often, but neither of us ever did anything to physically damage each other. We always ended up wrestling out of mutual respect instead of pummeling each other. Fights with other people turned out to be a different story, especially for Mickey, who lived in a big house across the street from the Ollie, the black junior high I had been run out of. I remember running through back yards, barely escaping a black gang that chased us to Mickey's house one night.

If you walked down the street and a gang of blacks approached on the same side, you had to walk straight through them. If you crossed to the other side of the street, they came after you. Your chances improved by walking right through, but sometimes things got worse, like one Sunday morning when Joey, Mickey, Dell, and I had a run-in near Mickey's house. We were on our way to a bar to buy beer on Sunday, an illegal act, both because of our age and because alcohol sales had been banned in Massachusetts on Sundays since earlier puritanical times. Aside from the money my friends carried, I had a pocket full of change.

A big gang of blacks appeared on the sidewalk in front of us. We walked through them until they surrounded us, then one of them walked into Mickey and held his hand out, demanding, "Give me a nickel, whitey."

"Fuck you; you ain't getting a nickel from me!" Mickey said, stepping back, preparing to fight. More blacks swarmed from every conceivable angle, prompting those closest to us to brandish straight razors, putting one to Dell's neck, one to Joey's, and one toward Mickey. If I ever had any doubts about being protected, this day proved it to be true. Of the four of us, I stood in the middle of this confrontation with a pocket bulging with change and nobody pulled a blade on me or threatened me. When Joey and Dell gave up their money, one of the blacks said, "You have until three to run, then you're fair game."

We bolted, carried by fear and adrenaline, then we separated until they gave up chasing us. They never got a cent from me or Mickey.

Joey, Dell, and Mickey became obsessed with stealing cars, which they called "hot boxes." Dell and Joey constantly tried to outdo each other with the magnitude of their exploits, often performing in front of crowds to see who could burn the most rubber. A popular version of this competition employed a technique called an RD, when they put the car into reverse and floored it, then slammed it into drive, keeping the foot on the gas to burn rubber for as long as they could without fishtailing into any of the parked cars lining the narrow street.

Sometimes they challenged each other to see who could steal the most cars in one day or who could steal one the fastest, the top speed being two minutes. Back then they stole cars by "popping" the ignition out with a dent puller and removing the tumblers, then putting it back in and starting it with a screwdriver. If they wanted a certain car but didn't want to spend the time getting it from a particular location, they stole a tow truck and towed it away. If they wanted to hustle a few bucks, they stole taxis and spent the day picking up fares at Logan Airport.

I learned how to steal a car before I knew how to drive one. One night, while hanging around with a friend's older brother who had just gotten out of jail at the age of twenty-one, he talked me into stealing a car. The plan called for me to drive up the street and pick him up so he could drive us to Quincy to meet some girls he knew.

I popped the ignition with a screwdriver, started it, and hit the car in front of me when I tried to pull out. The car stalled and the lights came on in front of the house. I jumped out and dove into the bushes. People came out seconds later, then the cops arrived. All this activity went on within a few feet of where I lay hidden. About forty-five minutes later, the cops left, the lights went out, and I bolted from the bushes, running up the street to find my friend waiting. This marked the first and last time I ever stole a car but not the last time I got into one.

I didn't want to be a car thief like my friends, because they always ended up getting busted, and as time passed their confrontations with the cops grew more violent. I could tell that the cops were getting fed up when Dell showed up on Alpha Road to hang out on someone's front porch with me. No sooner had he taken a seat when the cops came around the corner. Dell ducked into a hallway before the cops pulled up, asking me if I had seen him. I said no, but it didn't matter to the cop, who stepped out of the car and went straight to the hallway, where he found Dell. After a brief scuffle, the cop came out holding Dell by the arm. Dell held his cuffed hands in the air like a boxing champ, his face orange with mace. "Didn't see him, huh?" the cop said. I shrugged and didn't answer, watching them take my friend away.

In the beginning I found myself drawn to the thrill and temptation of a joyride, until I had the wildest ride imaginable with Dell one night. I had no idea how loaded he was when I got into the car with him, but I found out quickly when he informed me that we were going to the Youth Service Board, the juvenile detention center, to do a show that night. To get to the "Youthie," we had to drive through a big black section of Boston from Dorchester.

As soon as we arrived, Dell drove straight onto the front lawn and spun the car in circles, doing doughnut after doughnut, ripping up the grass. Lights went on everywhere and kids swarmed to the windows, cheering us on. Then the doors to the building slammed open and the "sirs" who guarded the kids came running toward us while Dell spun merrily away until the car stalled.

The men approached and swiftly closed in, reaching for the door handles when the car mercifully roared to life. Dell stomped on it and we fishtailed out of there, spewing chunks of turf and mud all over the sirs. Then Dell raced through the black part of town, hitting cars on both sides of the street. I kept yelling at him to stop and let me out, even though I would have been dead meat being the only white kid for miles. Dell drove back to Dorchester sideswiping and clipping cars the whole way, finally dropping me off on Alpha Road. I don't know how we didn't get caught, but that was the last time I took a ride in a hot box, especially with Dell.

Some months after that, he escaped from the Youth Service Board, but not before getting a load of rock salt in his side from a shotgun when he tried to steal an off-duty state trooper's car. I snuck him into the house when my mom wasn't home, then went to a department store and stole hair dye, a wallet, and a bandage. Together we bandaged his arm, dyed his blond hair black, and made him a false ID with a different name. Like lots of stray friends I dragged home, my mom took him in and let him stay. We found him a job where he worked regularly under his assumed name, and we ended up hanging out together every night for months.

On one of our last nights together, we threw a huge piece of sheet metal across the 20,000 volt third rail on the subway, sending up a huge explosion of sparks. Some lady saw us and screamed. The cops appeared in minutes and we barely escaped over a ten-foot barbed-wire-topped chain-link fence. Later that night Dell drank too much and got grabby with my girlfriend. We ended up in a confrontation that almost became physical until he left and stole a car. When a motorcycle cop pulled him over, Dell put the car in reverse and ran over the cop and his bike, getting himself busted.

Another time, a Boston motorcycle cop with the Tactical Police Force, otherwise known as the TPF, who rode a full-dressed Harley Davidson Electra Glide, chased Mickey and some other friends in a stolen car. The cop got hit in the face with a full can of beer that someone had thrown out the car window, knocking all his teeth out. The cops beat Mickey so bad with night sticks that his bandaged head

39

looked like a white turban. In an ironic twist, his mom, an emergency room nurse at Mass. General, saw him get rushed in that night.

The last I heard, a judge sentenced Mickey to a long stretch in one of the state pens for shooting a black kid in the face with a flare gun, point blank. Joey broadsided a bus, getting chased in a stolen car, killing an elderly woman. This sent him on his own long stretch in one of the state pens.

Dell told me over and over again that he was John Dillinger reincarnated, and truth be told, with his baby face, he looked like Dillinger. He also told me that he would never live to be twenty-one. At the age of eighteen, while I served in the air force, the cops cornered him behind the subway station where we had hung out and blew his brains out with a shotgun, following through by planting a fake gun on him.

He never made twenty.

NINE

Fear's Adrenaline

anging out on the steps at the top of Alpha Road kept us at odds with the district-eleven cops, who rousted us at least once a day. One slow summer day when we felt bored, we called them three times in a row, using different voices to report a gang fight. After calling, we ran to the steps and sat up top laughing while motorcycle cops followed by cruisers flew down Alpha Road, blue lights flashing, chasing nothing.

We came close to getting into real gang fights from time to time. In one incident, my friend Brian dated a girl who had a jealous former boyfriend. Three or four of us hung out on the Alpha Road steps one afternoon when a gang of eight or ten kids led by their jealous leader came running toward us. Everybody took off except me. I don't know why I stayed, but my actions confused our attackers, stopping them short.

"Why didn't you run with everybody else?" the leader said, confronting me.

"Why should I run?" I said. "I haven't done anything. I don't have any reason to run."

He sized me up, then looked to his gang, who all seemed equally baffled. Then he said, "You got a lot of balls. We were going to kick your ass, but you have a lot of balls compared to your friends. We're going to let you slide."

About a dozen of them caught up to us later. The jealous boyfriend pulled off his leather belt and chased my friend Brian, whipping him with the belt while the rest of the gang menaced the remaining three of us. One of my old school friends, Danny, pushed his way to the front of the gang and pointed at me, saying, "He's a friend of mine. Anybody fucks with him and I'll kick their ass."

Every time I relive that moment, I feel both blessed by Danny's friendship and protected, as if mysterious forces watched over me. Sometimes they came through my Mom, who had a knack for appearing when I faced trouble, like she did with Arnie, the bully, and the night at the Alpha Road steps, when she pulled up and ordered me and my brother into the car. Once in, we barreled down the street watching the cops appear in the rearview mirror, going after the gang on the steps. She had purchased a police radio that she listened to every night. After that, whenever she pulled up, we didn't argue.

I took to listening to the police radio when I could and often warned my friends when the cops went after them for drinking in the schoolyard. The cops chased us all the time; sometimes for a reason, other times for no apparent reason. I had many escape routes and I knew my way through every backyard on both sides of Alpha Road, across every navigable rooftop, through every fence hole, and I knew how to avoid every mean dog. I even made up my own obstacle course that ran up and down the whole block and I ran it as often as possible, sometimes leading groups of my friends. I had lots of close calls with the cops, but my fear and hyper-vigilance always saved me from getting caught.

The one night they caught me off guard I managed to slip away into the darkness when they grabbed my friends John and Tom for drinking in an abandoned garage. Though only fourteen, Tom was tall with black hair and a full beard that allowed him to buy alcohol unchallenged. Both he and John had been in the Boy Scouts with me and Mickey. John had three big brothers, Joe, Mike, and Tony. My older sister dated Mike and Tony, eventually falling in love with Tony, the oldest. John and his brothers had some resemblance to Elvis, which attracted my sister. They all had straight brown hair that matched their big brown eyes. John and I spent many nights drinking, playing cards, and smoking dope together.

In Dorchester the cops spent much of their time making the rounds to where gangs hung out, confiscating alcohol and telling the kids to get lost. They rarely arrested anyone unless that person started trouble. It became common knowledge that they made rounds before going to a cemetery for all night-drinking parties with their confiscated goods until Internal Affairs caught them in a sting operation, making a big scandal.

In the summer we went to Malibu Beach, where we jumped off the drawbridge where I had seen the kid get electrocuted. Joey always amazed us with his graceful swan dives from great heights, and he always seemed to go no more than a few feet below the surface before surfacing instantly. When we wanted a change from the bridges and colder salt water, we took the mass transit, then walked or hitchhiked to either Quincy or Milton to abandoned granite quarries filled with water from underground springs. They were rumored to be bottomless because numerous stolen cars and other missing things often disappeared into their depths. The water stayed warm during the summer and the quarries had lots of high cliffs to jump and dive from, some of them close to a hundred feet high with names like Bush and Nigger's Heaven.

They called the one jump Bush because you had to run hard and fast to leap over a bush from a high point into the water. If you didn't clear it, you smashed into the cliffs. Nigger's Heaven found its name from an upside down car sitting a few feet below the surface of the water with one of its doors opened on one side. To survive Nigger's Heaven, you had to dive into the spot between the angled open door and the car's body. Jimmy's, one of the highest jumps in all the quarries, brought one of the biggest thrills. If you didn't land right coming down from Jimmy's, you got hurt from the impact. Unlike Joey, I couldn't dive very well, so I never braved Nigger's Heaven, but after a long time staring down from the top of Jimmy's, I jumped, and from then on I jumped regularly for the adrenaline rush it never failed to provide.

During those summers, I had to be home by ten o'clock at night. I'd make my curfew and tell my mother "good night," going right upstairs to bed. Ten minutes later I climbed out my brother's window onto a roof and down a tree to meet Frankie, Joey the car thief's older brother. The two of us stayed out all night going to Dorchester's twenty-four-hour bowling alley, or we roamed the streets. One night a gang chased me and a big guy came close to grabbing me, but I flipped a trashcan into his path, sending him sprawling to the ground.

I was untouchable when fear's adrenaline guided my steps.

TEN

Sex Education and Subway Stations

ne of the few kids who did live on Alpha Road right next to the steps was a short Italian kid named Phil. Phil had brown hair and mischievous brown eyes that seemed to dare you to push the limits, and a sly smile that made you think he was always getting away with something. His father and uncles all had Mafia connections, and his mother drank hard with Joey and Frankie's mother, who was her best friend. The two of them ended up literally drinking themselves to death.

With an older brother, two older sisters, two younger sisters, and his mom being drunk all the time, Phil and I could do anything we wanted. Since they lived behind us, I had no problem getting my mom's permission to spend the night there. She had no idea how much freedom we had.

I drank a little before the age of thirteen, but I didn't have my first really good drunk until soon after turning fourteen. I ended up sleeping over at Phil's one drunken night, where I had my first ejaculation when I found myself fascinated with how good it felt to masturbate. I didn't know how far I could take it until I pushed past the limit to that moment of extreme pleasure that left me shocked, surprised, and enthralled with how things worked. Other than what I heard from my friends, that was the extent of my sex education until Dell took it upon himself to school me further.

He showed up one day with a cherub-faced girl with short brown hair named Noreen after escaping from the Youthie. I hid them out in the cellar until my mom busted us and ordered them upstairs, where she gave them the third degree while feeding them. Dell found a place for Noreen to stay and invited me over a couple of weeks later. Soon after I got there, he went into a back bedroom with her and came out a short while later, saying, "Do you want to get laid?"

His unexpected question caught me off guard and I didn't know what to say or do.

"She's back there waiting for you," he said matter-of-factly.

"Sure," I said, not knowing how else to respond.

He sent me back to the bedroom, where I found Noreen waiting for me under the covers with her panties off. I didn't quite know what to do, but I knew what was supposed to go where, so I dropped my pants down around my ankles, climbed into the bed, and did the deed, reaching climax in what I'm sure was record time. The whole experience felt surreal and embarrassing, but it felt good.

With the exception of his younger sisters, everybody in Phil's family drank all the time. I got drunk with him often. Sometimes his older sister joined us and Phil would try to get me to have sex with her when she supposedly passed out, but I couldn't do anything with an audience and it just didn't feel right.

My brother discovered big Jim's hidden black-and-white eight millimeter stag films and decided to have a special showing. We scored some alcohol, hooked school, and charged fifty cents a head for the screening. Now my sex education became complete, consisting of what I heard from my friends, my own drunken self-discovery, stag films, and sex with Noreen.

Phil moved to another part of Dorchester, closer to Southie, where his father bought a three-story house with a garage and a pool table. I spent many days and nights there as part of the family. Phil managed to get us jobs pumping gas, though neither one of us had reached the legal working age. We showed up almost every day, pumping gas, fixing flats, running errands, and doing whatever else we could do. Sometimes on Saturday nights the gas stations in the area took turns covering the garage-door windows. Cases of beer were brought in and the white brick wall at the back of the garage became the screen for eight-millimeter stag movies.

When the guys at the gas station had problems with the owners of a restaurant across the street, they asked me and Phil to help even the score. While they kept watch, we followed their instructions. After popping the hood on the guy's car, we took off his air cleaner and put nuts and bolts down his carburetor, then we worked the choke so the metal fell down into the engine, which eventually caused it to seize. Someone told the restaurant owners that Phil and I had ruined their car, so they hired guys to break our legs. When Phil's father found out, he and some of his friends paid the restaurant owner a visit that resulted in the leg-breakers being called off.

The gas station didn't pay much, so before long we took money from the cash register on a regular basis, using schemes like pumping eight dollars worth of gas and ringing it up as two. One Saturday night after a big haul, we called a cab and talked the driver into buying us a case of beer and some cigars for a generous tip. With money flowing freely, we had him take us all over Dorchester, at one point driving by the gang at the Alpha Road steps. For an added tip, he burned rubber to the cheers of the gang. That night gave me my first taste of what it felt like to be a high roller.

I took the subway home from Savin Hill station on the nights I worked late because it took too long to walk or ride my bike. The quickest way to Savin Hill took me through blocks of empty streets bordered by rows of vacant factories and warehouses where many a cab driver had been robbed, often ending up stabbed, shot, or beaten and left for dead. I always hustled to a lot bordering the subway platform, where I hopped the fence, jumped over the third rail, and walked up the steps at the end of the deserted platform.

I sat alone on a bench there one night when an older graying man in a long jacket and a rumpled suit came down the platform and sat beside me, striking up a conversation. At first his words sounded light and friendly, then it became personal when he asked, "Do you have a girlfriend?"

"Yeah, as a matter of fact, I have a few."

"You ever thought about being with men?"

"No," I said, putting some distance between us. "Girls are way more exciting to me than men."

"Do you want to go back to my apartment with me?" He asked, pointing his thumb in the opposite direction from mine.

"No, thanks," I said, waving him off. "I need to get home."

"Are you sure?" he asked again. I watched his excitement increase when he saw his train coming.

"No!" I said with more force.

When his train rolled into the station, he stood and grabbed for my crotch. I jumped up and punched him in the chest, knocking him into the train before it rolled to a stop. He bounced off the side and stumbled onto the train when the doors opened, clearly shaken. Then the doors hissed shut behind him, whisking him away. I had heard about the predators, but this was my first confrontation with one.

The South Station men's room had a reputation as the biggest hangout for old queers trying to pick up young boys. If you've ever been assaulted by the smell of urine steaming from a hot rock in a campfire, you know the stench of the subway restrooms these guys hung out in. In my mid-teens some of my friends decided to prey on the predators, offering to let the old queers give a teenager a blow job for fifty bucks. Whoever accepted the offer found themselves beaten and robbed. I never took part in any of it. As time passed, I heard that my hustler friends changed their violent ways and became prostitutes, which proved to be more lucrative than robbing.

The first time I rode the subway, around the age of six, I hung onto the pole in the middle of the car, afraid of falling out of the rattling doors that hissed open at each stop. Newer, more modern cars soon replaced the old rattletraps, giving new life to the subway, which thrived as an integral part of life in Boston. In our last few years in Dorchester, my brother, myself, and the Alpha Road gang migrated to Shawmut Station, the second to the last subway stop at the end of the

Red Line before Ashmont Station, where we joined with more friends from another gang.

Standing in front of Shawmut Station, we could hear the trains coming underground and feel the vibration from below in our feet. When the train hissed into the station, the big heavy metal doors at the front of the building blew open as if pushed by invisible crowds, followed by real crowds exiting the subway. If we timed it right, we could run through the open doors to hop the turnstiles and run down the stairs and onto the train before the guy in the booth could do anything about it.

Aside from hopping the turnstiles, we hopped the third rail at outdoor stations, crossed the tracks, and came up at the end of the platform. One of the neighborhood kids tripped and fell across the third rail onto the tracks at Shawmut, frying from twenty thousand volts like the metal sheet that Dell and I had thrown across the tracks. His death put a good scare into all of us, but we still hopped the rail, tempting death, even in the underground stations that had no escape if a train came. Shawmut also had the notoriety of being the station where the cops blew Dell's brains out with a shotgun.

Late one night I came back to Shawmut on the train after a big egg fight in Phil's neighborhood with one egg left. I found Gook and Yackie, a couple of the guys who always hung out in front of Shawmut, playing cards on the sidewalk. Yackie had been nicknamed because he had problems saying his own name, Jackie. Small and frail with a humpback, a neck brace, and problems with his legs, Yackie treated everyone decent. Gook, an athlete bigger than Yackie, always bullied him, especially at cards, and I'm sure Gook cheated him. This night I walked out of the station to the sound of Gook yelling and bullying Yackie, so I kept my stride and smashed the egg I had hard, breaking it into Gook's open mouth, saying, "Shut the fuck up and leave Yackie the fuck alone."

Gook's eyeballs bugged out of his head and everybody who saw it loved it. Gook's treatment toward Yackie changed after that, giving me a great sense of self-satisfaction.

I met my mother at Shawmut station every day to walk her home so she wouldn't get mugged after four black guys beat my friend Billy's mother into a coma with chains. I walked my sisters home from time to time to watch over them too. One day, when some bigger kids chased my little sister home from school, I couldn't get out of the house quickly enough, so I picked them off with a BB gun from a second-story window, scoring a couple of stinging hits that sent them screaming.

Once on the subway, we could joyride all over the city, changing routes and destinations whenever we felt like it. More often than not, the subways held adventure, like the day Joey and I sat at Field's Corner station, waiting for the train. Two bigger kids threatened us and tried to take our money until Joey recognized a bigger friend of ours, tipping the odds in our favor, three to two. We took all of the would-be thieves' money and terrorized them for a number of stops before throwing them off the train.

A gang of us took the subway to my first rock concert to see Grand Funk Railroad. We took over a subway car and passed around bottles of wine and reefers. At the concert I sat up behind the stage over an exit guarded by the cops. Every time someone passed me a burned-down roach, I dropped it onto the cops below.

ELEVEN

Outer and Inner Space

never liked school, even from the beginning. Trying to avoid kindergarten, I went outside one day, hoping my mom wouldn't find me. I resisted her calls until she urged me to hurry so I could see Alan Shepard make history when he lifted off into space on television. Her lure worked, and from that moment on I had a consuming fascination with space travel and the desire to be an astronaut.

By the time I reached my early teens, any money I acquired I spent on mail-order model rocket kits. When they came I lagged until my mom left for work. Then I skipped school and spent hours alone, building rockets and dreaming of space flight. I even gave up the prettiest girls in the neighborhood because of my obsession with rockets.

I had many failed launches and a few successes, the best of them being a spider that survived its flight in a see-through payload container. I followed the space program religiously and knew every rocket, what kind of fuel it used, and what type of space capsule it carried. I also kept most of the newspapers from the Apollo project, especially the full copies of all of the Boston and New York newspapers that came out on the day Apollo Eleven landed on the moon. I spent hours drawing up plans for a Lunar Module Simulator that I fantasized building out of plywood in our cellar so I could spend a week in it, living on Space Food Sticks and Tang, two popular consumer products that came out of the space program.

In my mid-teens I found myself at a crossroads between the financial realities of life in Dorchester and the dreams I had of being an astronaut. I felt my life following two paths, one legitimate and the other criminal. I had never been arrested for anything, so I began to think that my illegal endeavors could finance my legitimate pursuits, allowing me to make it in the world. My life had become a paradox of good and bad that battled inside of me for years to come; the good nurtured by my mother's loving honesty, the bad stemming from my old man's raging insanity, con-artist persona, and affinity for getting loaded on whatever he could find, including cough medicine. I still carried my life's ambition to be a successful criminal, only I never wanted to hurt anyone. So far I had succeeded. Deep down I wanted to do good in the world, but I had no resources. The only path I could conceive of mingled somewhere amid Dorchester's milieu of stolen goods, robberies, and scams, which were all accepted realities that became second nature.

Another ambition that evolved into one of the driving forces of my life became the desire to try as many new experiences as possible. I recognized this as another facet of the urge to fly out into space as an astronaut, only this one pointed toward the infinite reaches of inner space. While hanging out at the Alpha Road steps, we took turns putting our hands behind our knees, squatting down with deep exhales and standing up, inhaling ten times in a row, holding our breath on the last inhale while someone held us in a bear hug until we passed out. I loved the fuzzing out sensation of losing consciousness; in fact, I was discovering that I loved anything that altered my consciousness.

By the time I was fourteen, I smoked a pack and a half of cigarettes a day and drank, mostly on Friday and Saturday nights. With a dollar I could talk Obie the change thief or someone else into buying me a bottle of Boone's Farm Apple or Strawberry Hill wine. If we couldn't find someone to buy for us, we hung around outside the liquor store asking the men who went in, offering them a tip. Cheap wine brought a good buzz for a buck. Aside from Boone's Farm, we drank Mogen David, otherwise known as Mad Dog, Ripple, Yago Spanada, Mateus, and Thunderbird, which had its own street verse.

"What's the word?

Thunderbird.

What's the price?

Thirty twice.

Who drinks the most?

Us white folks."

Two bucks bought a six pack of beer or a half-pint of Bacardi Rum and a quart of Coke, which soon became my favorite. After drinking some of the Coke from the quart, I added the rum and walked around drinking from the Coke bottle without getting hassled by the cops. Though alcohol led me into many strange situations, it only took me so far, and the farther it took me, the less I remembered and the more I paid for it the day after.

One of my friends from the Alpha Road gang came to the steps one day saying he had smoked pot with a kid in school and urged me to try it. It didn't take much to convince me. Smoking marijuana sounded exotic compared to drinking. The first time I smoked it, another one of my friends surprised us with some hashish, so I smoked pot and hashish my first time and loved the buzz. When someone asked one of my friends how he felt, the response of "pleasantly wrecked" became the giggle phrase that defined that night. After smoking, a gang of us walked to a pizza parlor and discovered the joy of eating pizza while stoned.

We soon had a connection in Dorchester. Five dollars bought a nickel bag, consisting of a bank envelope with enough pot for a half a dozen good-sized joints with no stems or seeds, an incredible bang for the buck with lots of high to share and no hangover. After feeling how different pot was from alcohol, I had an overwhelming desire to try anything else that might alter my perception. I don't know who came up with the idea, but a bunch of us decided to try sniffing glue. With a can of Weldwood contact cement and paper lunch bags, we found safe places to pour dollops of glue into our bags, then we put them to our faces and breathed in the intoxicating fumes. Hyperventilating and passing out had nothing on sniffing glue. Someone said that sniffing it killed millions of brain cells, but we didn't care. Nobody knew what to believe, but we all loved the experience, which I look back on as my first psychedelic journeys.

I have a vivid memory of one of my first experiences floating up through the ceiling of a third-floor apartment and rising higher over the rooftops in an exquisite dreamlike out-of-body ecstasy. I floated weightless, riding the winds before coming down through the roof again, gradually becoming aware of myself back in the room. Looking down at the rug, I saw shifting patterns spelling out words and messages that I couldn't decipher.

Every time I sniffed glue I found myself taken away to dreamlike fantasy lands where the normal rules of time, space, and being didn't apply. My imagination literally soared. I felt so powerfully drawn to these experiences that I sensed myself slipping too far over some invisible boundary, flirting with a mysterious dark addiction. This became apparent to me when I came up from the cellar one night, zoned out with a bag of glue under my jacket, to find my mother questioning me. I could barely respond, but I told her I felt sick and needed to go to bed. She didn't pursue it, but I knew she sensed something was wrong.

My friend Billy, a dark-eyed Portuguese kid with curly brown hair who sniffed glue with me, had a real edge to him. He had been thrown out of public school in the sixth grade and forced to go to a military school instead of jail for stealing his poor mom's car. Anytime he got busted, his mom would say, "My Billy do nothing. It's those boy he hang around with." In reality her Billy often turned out to be the biggest troublemaker out of all of us.

Billy's mother liked me because I respected her and I had been a Boy Scout, but I freaked her out when she came home one day to find me and Billy sailing on the glue-fumed breezes. I came back to my body in the room, looking up from my glue bag, drooling, while Billy's mother yelled at us. It always shocked me to hear the way he talked to his mother because I had been taught to respect mine. He always yelled, "Fuck you, Ma!" and degraded her with more expletives.

I slipped out the front door and took off while they argued. Things never felt the same with her after that, but she still liked me because I never disrespected her and it bothered me deeply when Billy did.

Sniffing glue led me to one of the most terrifying experiences of my life one hot summer night when Billy and I went to a department store in Field's Corner to buy some glue to sniff. They wouldn't sell us any, so we went out front and stood by the doorway trying to figure out what to do.

Staccato explosions popped off behind me, scaring the shit out of me. I thought someone had lit off M-80s or cherry bombs until I spun around and saw a cop a few feet from me, blasting away at two guys with his .38 while they shot back with sawed-off shotguns. The robbers ran past me and the cop shot one in the leg as he passed. I dropped to the ground beneath the front window and watched the havoc unfold, feeling as if I had become part of a movie.

When the guy took the hit in front of me, a lady ran away from him, screaming as she dove to the pavement, sending her bags of groceries scattering in all directions. The cop's side bled from wounds from the shotgun's ricochet, but his injuries appeared minor. Someone took the bag of money he had been carrying and secured it while cops poured into the lot, blue lights flashing.

I felt numb as the cops hustled us into the store to get statements. Then a guy came running in from the parking lot with a sawed-off shotgun that the wounded robber had dropped. He carried it using a key through the trigger guard and dropped it when he came in, but it didn't go off.

I was shaking when they herded us out after we gave our statements, and I walked out with the wounded cop carrying the sawed-off shotgun behind me. He dropped it again and it went off. The concussion pushed me forward from below my knees, making me think that my legs had been blown off.

When I told one of the cops on the scene what happened, he told me to get lost and mind my own business. By this time I shook even more and I walked home in a daze. My mom sensed something right away. When I told her, Jim had her take me to our doctor, thinking we could get a lot of money if we sued. The doctor found superficial pinhole wounds in my ankles from the pulverized concrete.

Jim pushed to sue the cops. I talked to a lawyer, running through what we would say in our testimony. He asked us what we were doing at the store, and we said, "Trying to buy some glue." He studied us for a second, then said, "No, no, you weren't trying to buy glue. You were buying a new shirt, right?"

A few weeks later, the shotgun, the key piece of evidence, disappeared, which brought me relief because my heart didn't feel right about suing. The intensity of that experience told me I had become too lost in the spell of the glue, so I decided to stop.

One afternoon, close to a dozen of my friends decided to sniff glue at the transit, an asphalt place bordered by chain-link fences and houses where the subway trains ran underground. They begged me to go, but I had made my mind up, so I watched them all go, staying behind by myself. One of them showed up about forty-five minutes later to tell me that everyone had gotten busted. Joey had been so far gone he laughed at the cops when they arrested him, seeing them as giant chickens. My friends told me they hadn't even realized they had been busted until they got their bearings in the back of a squad car.

I have no doubt that something connected to my intuition watched over and guided me through those lessons, protecting me the way it had many times before. Escaping the bust gave me irrefutable proof that I had made the right decision in quitting. The glue had indeed been taking me to too many weird places.

TWELVE

High School, Race Relations, and Becoming What You Hate

efore I turned fifteen, I qualified for a summer work program for low-income kids, making thirty-five dollars a week for forty hours of work as a day-camp counselor for a bunch of screaming, half-wild little ghetto kids. Empowered by my newfound paycheck, I took my younger cousin to downtown Boston to have some fun and spend some money. While walking on Boylston Street, we passed the edge of the Combat Zone, a two-block section on the edge of downtown full of X–rated movie theaters, peep shows, and strip joints populated by pimps, hookers, hustlers, drug dealers, scammers, and muggers. As we passed, two bigger black kids blocked our way, confronting us.

The biggest one towered over us, demanding, "Give me all your money, white boy."

I reached into my back pocket, pulled out a small mace canister, and stuck it in the big one's face, saying, "You want to take my money, nigger? Come and get it!"

"What's that, tear gas?" he said, backing away.

"You want to find out, motherfucker? Come on!" I lunged at him, stomping my foot.

He and his friend took off running and I hustled my cousin around the corner, ducking into Madam Tussaud's Wax Museum on Park Street. No sooner had I paid our admission when a gang of seven or eight black kids led by our would-be muggers went storming up the street past the front window. My cousin and I spent a couple of hours touring the museum, then slipped across the street to Park Street station and took the subway home.

When summer ended I followed in my brother's footsteps after taking the "Tech test" to qualify for Boston Technical High School, a mostly white boys' high school that took kids from all over the city. Tech was located in Roxbury, Malcolm X's stomping grounds in the heart of Boston's biggest black section. We took the Washington Street bus with a dollar for car fare; ten cents each way for the bus, thirty cents to buy a school lunch, and fifty cents for a pack of smokes. Whenever I found a way to sneak on the bus, I saved ten or twenty cents that I could buy an after-school treat with. In my freshman year, I entered one of my rockets in the science fair, which immortalized me in the year book. It also marked the end of my rocket adventures. Smoking pot and chasing after girls now competed for my attention.

Attending a mostly white boys' high school in the middle of Boston's black neighborhood had its challenges. Race riots and forced bussing in the late sixties caused us to miss school for weeks when they shut everything down on account of the violence. Even though we stayed safe in numbers, we still had confrontations with the blacks who remained a constant threat throughout most of my childhood. No one knew what to do about them and the problems they caused. Big Jim, my mother's truck-driver husband, had his own solution that embodied Dorchester's prevailing attitude: "If I were president, I'd take all the niggers, put them all on boats, and ship them all back to Africa. When they get halfway there, I'd torpedo them."

One day, while I was sneaking a cigarette in a fourth-floor lavatory with a few other guys, some older black kids yelled at us from below before heaving big rocks up at the window. I couldn't believe they were dumb enough to stand below and do that, but they succeeded in smashing through the big window. We threw the rocks and smashed glass back down at them, along with one of the lavatory sinks, before teachers came.

I began to grasp the truth of "You will become what you hate" in my freshman year. Where I lived and who I lived with made me a racist, and I hated bullies, yet I didn't realize that I had become a bully myself until I picked on a quiet kid in my freshman class at Tech. His brother, a senior, came and talked to me with a couple of his friends one day. He came across cool and didn't threaten me or get bad with me. He simply asked me if I could stop picking on his little brother because I scared him and he didn't want any trouble with me. I liked the older brother's approach, so I backed off and left the kid in my class alone, primarily because his older brother had confronted the situation while treating me with respect and I admired him for it.

While racial tensions escalated, Tech held its ground in Boston's biggest black neighborhood. Hardly any black kids attended. Everyone said that the niggers were either too lazy or too stupid to pass the Tech test. One defining incident at the beginning of my freshman year showed me the ignorance of this "wisdom."

A couple of days into the school year, before anybody really knew anyone else, we walked by the gym where some seniors played basketball during a class change. A ball came bouncing out the gym door to me, followed by a senior who said, "Give me the ball!" in a threatening manner. Then another one called out, "No, give it to me." The first one grew more menacing and threatened me, so I threw the ball to the one with better manners.

The first one came at me and we got into a fight. Twenty-seven white classmates ran away scared while Marcel and Willie, the only two black guys in our class, stood their ground and backed me up. The big basketball-playing senior kept trying to throw me down while I grabbed onto his shirt. Every time he tried to throw me, I hung on, ripping his shirt and popping his buttons all over the place. When the teachers charged in to break it up, I ducked into the crowd while the dork with the shredded shirt got dragged off and suspended.

After that Willie, Marcel, and I became tighter than the rest of the cowards. Willie and I liked to turn each other on with good weed. I rolled my joints in my bedroom at night and kept them in my cigarette pack. Willie used to sit in geometry class rolling big joints behind his books while I watched, both entertained and amazed. When he finished, he buried the joints deep in his afro. After class he'd grab me and Marcel and the three of us would smoke a joint by the open classroom window after everyone had gone.

Between Bruce, Willie, and Marcel, I began to see the ignorance of prejudice. I had initially accepted it because, with the exception of my mother, that's what life taught me. I realized that I hated blacks because everybody else did, though I did have personal reasons, like getting so many knives pulled on me. Like everything else I had been taught, I did question it. So far three black guys had shown me different.

THIRTEEN

The Black Threat

Over time my sister broke up with my drinking buddy John's big brother Tony. With the Viet-Nam war in full swing, Tony went into the army. Halfway through his hitch, he went AWOL while his younger brother Mike, who was serving in the Marines, got wounded and poisoned. John and I used to visit him at his apartment to buy hashish. After splitting with my sister, Tony got married, had a kid, and divorced. After her split with Tony, my sister fell into the darkest hell when she became trapped in the black vortex of a biker named Jo Jo, one of the sickest, most sadistic people to walk the streets of Dorchester. More than twice my sister's age, Jo Jo got her pregnant before she reached seventeen.

At first he overwhelmed and seduced her with his fancy car and full-dressed Harley Davidson. The first time she spoke up in a conversation with his friends, he punched her in the face, nearly knocking her teeth out. When she tried to leave him, he told her that he and his friends would kill our family, so my sister caved in fear and the jaws of his trap sprang shut.

While brutalizing my sister, Jo Jo faced a three-to-four-year stretch in Walpole, the same prison my father had done time in. My sister told us that he had a job working offshore on an oil rig. I had no idea what was going on back then because everything was hidden from me, but for seven years Jo Jo's presence brought darkness and tragedy into our lives. He died, leaving behind lifelong scars from the damage and abuse he inflicted on my sister and my two nieces. In spite of my mother's efforts to help, ruled by terror, my sister gave birth to my oldest niece and moved out of our house to live with Jo Jo's mother while he served his three-year stretch in the big house.

A fifteen-year-old girl who cleaned Jo Jo's apartment had a disagreement with her older brother over the work she did cooking for Jo Jo, so Jo Jo called him into the apartment to talk things over. When the brother came in, Jo Jo handcuffed him to a table and beat him with a chain, then forced him to eat dog food. After getting arrested and charged, Jo Jo beat my sister's shins black and blue with empty soda bottles, permanently damaging her veins, telling her, "There's more where that came from if you testify against me."

When my sister gave birth to my oldest niece, big Jim, my mother's husband, took on the nickname of Grampy, which pleased me because I could never bring myself to refer to him as my stepfather. By this time I resented Jim's laziness and the way he treated my mother, but we kept an uneasy love-hate friendship for the sake of my mother.

Jim drove an eighteen-wheeler and sometimes snuck me in to do long hauls with him, which helped our bond. Sometimes we hung out together, and when I grew older, we frequented some of the same bars. To his credit, he did help me out a few times. When a nutty Italian kid named Stevie kept all our earnings after I shoveled snow with him, Jim took me to his house, knocked on the door, and confronted him in front of his mother until he forked over the money he owed me. Another time a guy grabbed my brother for something he didn't do, then called the cops and made an ugly scene. I ran and got Jim, who confronted the cop and the guy, saving my brother. I'm sure a big reason my mother married him was because he did protect us, but

with three kids from his first marriage, child support, and
didn't provide for us. My mom carried most of the load, and I
him for that.

Our landlord was one of the biggest slumlords in Dorchester. N
mom noticed that the old battle ax had stopped cashing the rent checks,
so she started sending them via registered mail. When the landlord
tried to evict us for nonpayment of the rent, my mom produced the
registered mail receipts along with pictures of the holes in the ceilings
and the furnace that broke down more than it worked. We spent many
cold winter mornings huddled around the kitchen stove with the oven
door open for heat. The judge ruled that we didn't have to pay any
more rent until the problems were fixed. Soon afterward my mom and
Jim made a down payment on a house in a small town close to the
Rhode Island border.

Small-town life with a bunch of hicks was the last thing in the
world I wanted, but moving out of Dorchester probably saved my life.
The violence had grown to the point that if I walked down the street
after dark and a car approached and slowed, I dove into the bushes or
bolted down an alley for fear of getting shot.

Shortly before moving, my mom, niece, and I drove down Harvard
Street, passing the same place the black gang with straight razors had
jumped me, Joey, Dell, and Mickey. A dog darted out in front of the
car and my mother hit it, then it ran off. Concerned and wanting to do
the right thing, she stopped to try to find the owner. A gang of blacks
confronted her. When she asked them who owned the dog, they gave
her belligerent answers. She pleaded with them, telling them that she
only wanted to do the right thing, but they grew more belligerent,
saying things like "White bitch tried to kill the dog" and other more
threatening statements. I felt apprehensive, not only for my mom but
for my two-year-old niece. I called out, "Get back in the car, Mom,"
but she persisted, trying to find out who owned the dog.

The mob grew and their menacing insults increased with their
numbers. I called to her again, but she didn't seem to hear me. I felt
as if violence would erupt any second, so I reached down and grabbed
the crook lock, a heavy sliding steel apparatus that hooked over the
steering wheel and under the brake pedal to prevent theft. Swinging its

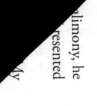

ngth hard slid it out another foot and a half to its ..., making it an excellent weapon.

... car, I moved between my mom and the angry ...rook lock above my shoulder like a baseball bat, ... first one of you motherfuckers who wants part ... me and get it." Then I said, "Get back in the car, ... he danger registered and she went back to the passenger side. I backed up to the driver's door, hopped in, and drove off, leaving the cursing mob behind.

Harvard Street remained a tough area where large gangs of blacks walked out in front of cars, making people stop. Then they dragged the driver and passengers out of the car to beat and rob them. Months after moving out of Dorchester, I drove through there with Jim. Sure enough, a gang of blacks stepped out in front of the car. I reached down to grab the crook lock, but Jim stomped on the gas and headed for the crowd, chasing them onto the sidewalk. He drove up over the curb, barely missing the last of them as they jumped into a storefront entrance.

"Nice move," I said, feeling myself shaking.

"Son of a bitch. I missed," he said, driving on as if nothing out of the ordinary had happened.

A week before we moved, a friend's little brother who worked at a convenience store told me he had left the back door wedged open. I went in that night, taking boxes of candy, chips, all kinds of junk food, and a few bucks that we split. I hauled my loot home, packed my stuff, and left Dorchester with a good haul. In a case of instant karma, while we were moving out, someone stole my bicycle for the third time, along with some of my mom's stuff.

On the eve of my sixteenth birthday, my friends threw me a great party. On the morning after the party that I never wanted to end, Jim brought home his company's eighteen-wheeler and we moved out of Dorchester to a small town near Rhode Island.

Someone set the old house on fire soon after we moved out.

FOURTEEN

R-E-S-P-E-C-T and My First Encounter with Keystone Cops

didn't know what to expect from a small town after living in Dorchester, except boondocks, hicks, and boredom. Part of me liked the idea of living near the woods, where I could walk and get away from people, but most of me missed the frenetic, nonstop hustle of Dorchester. I didn't know how I would be able to relate to small-town "country boys," all of whom seemed rich to me because their parents owned the houses they lived in, which was a rarity in Dorchester.

I had hooked school so much in my sophomore year at Boston Tech that I had to complete my junior year in a sophomore home room. If I passed all of my classes, I would go into a senior home room the next school year. This arrangement complicated my already painful transfer from an all-boys inner-city high school to a co-ed high school in the sticks. The contrasts amazed me. After more than a decade of broken, battered wooden desks in Boston's ancient turn-of-the-century red-brick buildings, the modern, sprawling one-floor facility with its huge windows felt new and expansive. The difference in school lunches told the same story. For thirty cents Boston public school lunches gave you a small plate with little variety and plastic forks and knives so people couldn't stab each other. The forks always broke in the rock-hard meatloaf. My new school had full-sized plates, real metal silverware, and a wider variety of more palatable food.

The guidance counselor in my new high school told me I wouldn't be able to graduate in the next year because I fell a quarter of a point short in credits. When my mom heard this, she paid him a determined visit that put me back in the lineup to graduate in 1973, as originally promised.

On the second day of school, I heard low murmurs and whispers behind me, followed by laughter. When it continued I realized that a kid I thought of as a spoiled rich punk, whose father was the town's selectman, was making fun of me and getting laughs at my expense. I waited one day until he had everyone going, then I stood, turned, looked him in the eye, and said, "Look, Alice, you got something to say to me, say it to my face. Otherwise shut the fuck up or I'll shut you up." I stared at him while the hushed room felt suspended in timelessness and the glee faded from his eyes and was replaced by fear. I turned back to my chair and sat down, going about my business. After that he wanted to be my best buddy and even offered to carry my books. I humored him until he backed off, kept out of my way, and gave me the respect I demanded. From that day forward, everyone else respected me too.

My older sister had moved out to live-in hell with Jo Jo's mother. My brother, who had just graduated from Boston Tech, moved out of Dorchester with us, but he worked in Boston, which meant a long commute. The small-town atmosphere made him stir crazy, so he moved back to Dorchester, leaving me and my ten-year-old younger sister behind.

The first few kids who came to our door struck me as strange and out of touch until I discovered that the kid who lived two houses down from us shared my homeroom along with his sister, whom I liked, and best of all, he liked to smoke pot. We smoked and he took me to his friend's house; an exceptionally strange kid with a reputation for sniffing gasoline in his basement. In spite of the godsend of pot, I felt I had been punished by being banished to the boondocks with strange people who would drive me insane with boredom.

A few nights later, I met some younger kids who wanted to steal batteries from the school buses at the edge of our housing development. Their initiative and enthusiasm appealed to me. Though our attempt to steal batteries failed, our mutual interest created a lasting bond. I had a difference of opinion with one of the younger kids on that first night, and he made the mistake of threatening me with his big brothers. I told him to bring them on, and if they wanted to jump me all at once, I'd be waiting with a two-by-four to see who was the bravest and the baddest.

I met his "big brothers" a couple of nights later and we became instant friends. I soon discovered that the little punk had a reputation for running his mouth. Terry, the biggest one in the gang, who looked bearish with long brown hair and a full beard, wasn't even his brother. His real brother, Jimmy, looked skinny and posed no threat to me. Jimmy knew his little brother had a big mouth.

Terry and the gang were in the process of building a "fort" in the woods, complete with framing, a raised floor, roof, and a wood-burning stove fashioned from a steel drum. The fort gave us a place to drink and get high, and it gave us privacy and warmth in the winter. My brother became involved with us in the beginning, and the new gang loved to see us fighting and literally bouncing off the walls.

Through all my years growing up in Dorchester, I had been chased by the cops or had some kind of run-in with them on an almost daily basis, but I had never been arrested. If the Boston cops caught us drinking, they told us to get lost. If they were pricks, they made us pour out our drinks and confiscated the rest for themselves. This is how I understood the rules. Little did I know how petty and obnoxious bored small-town cops could be.

On the eve of my seventeenth birthday, my new friends and I bought a couple of cases of beer and drove to the next town to meet some girls and go to a sand pit to party without bothering anyone. Soon after we parked, the cops arrived, and I instinctively took off running to the top of a sand hill. They called me down while talking to my friends, and since they seemed low key, I obliged, especially since none of us had hardly drank a drop.

To my dismay, they arrested all of us. My buddies were over seventeen, which made them adults according to the law, yet they couldn't drink. These small-town cops arrested me four hours before I turned seventeen for possession of alcohol. Every fiber of my being raged at the idiocy and ignorance of a society that made military service mandatory. In four hours I could be drafted, taught to kill, and sent to Viet-Nam, but I could still be arrested for drinking alcohol.

No wonder I hated the system and didn't want any part of it.

While my friends scurried to arrange bail, the cops processed the girls and me as juveniles, calling our parents. My mom told me the details of the call.

"This is the police. We have your son under arrest for possession."

"Possession of what?"

"Alcohol."

"Is this a crank phone call?"

"No."

"You're not serious, are you?"

"We found your son in possession of alcohol and he was with some younger girls, and you know what could have happened with these girls and alcohol. We suggest sending your son away to the Youth Service Board for the weekend."

"Send him away? What's the matter with you? Don't tell me what could have happened with my son and those girls, and don't tell me he was drunk, because he only left here an hour ago. Where are you located? I'll be right down to come and get him."

She came, picked me up, and brought me home, both of us puzzling over the overbearing small-town attitude the cops had. My friends pooled their money and paid to get one of them out. He soon returned with a handful of crisp new counterfeit twenties to bail everyone else out. I felt vindicated after hearing this, feeling there was justice in the world after all in spite of the crime-busting efforts of the Keystone cops.

Back in Dorchester, my brother and some of our friends started riding motorcycles. Most of them bought Honda 350s and I ached to ride one myself, but I couldn't afford it. Some of my new country friends had dirt bikes, so I got to do some motocross riding. Wayne, a short, wiry kid with long, straight brown hair and questioning brown eyes, bought a Honda 305 that he let all of us ride. I'd ride his Honda into Dorchester to buy pot and other substances from people I knew and could trust.

In a short period of time, Wayne and I went into business selling pot. After years in Dorchester selling stolen car parts, fireworks, and other hot goods, dealing drugs felt natural. I went back to Dorchester as much as I could, usually staying at a friend's apartment, hanging out with the old gang, drinking, and smoking lots of pot through gas masks, hookahs, joints, water pipes, and various other inventions. Our choices of cannabis improved, ranging from low-grade Mexican to Jamaican, Columbian, Thai Stick, hashish, and other rare imports.

Meanwhile, Dell, Mickey, and Joey fell deeper into the mire of the system through wilder, more defiant acts against the cops. They upped the ante with every new exploit. Mickey had someone after him and needed a place to hide out, so I took him out to the sticks. As it turned out, one of my new small-town friends had spent a weekend in the Youth Service Board with Mickey, who had tried to take his dessert. They were cool about it and let it go when they realized they had me as a friend in common. Mickey stayed with us until things blew over, then I took him back to Dorchester and never saw him again.

FIFTEEN

Turn On, Tune In, and Freak Out

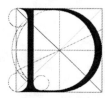uring my senior year, I skipped school at least eighty days out of a 180-day year. I mainly went to school to sell pot and drugs. When I was finished selling in the boy's room, I gave what I had left to my friend Alice to sell in the girl's room.

My best buddy, Terry, who eventually married Alice, told me he had tried LSD. His description of it piqued my interest along with a healthy fear that added to its attraction. One winter night, Terry brought some supposed LSD. I kept thinking I got off after taking it as I watched snow flurries coming down in the street lights, trying to convince myself that I was seeing colors and traces, but nothing more ever came of it.

It took going back to Dorchester to connect with the real thing— and connect I did, in a way that shattered any preconceived ideas I had about the true nature of reality. During the summer I escaped back to

Dorchester to spend a weekend with my buddy Mike, who had moved in with some friends who had connections for lots of different drugs. Mike had access to all the cannabis anybody could ever want, and now he had discovered LSD, which he shared with me one life-changing summer night.

We went to Wollaston Beach in Quincy, a suburb south of Boston, where he tapped out one hit of acid from a small vial full of four-way Orange Barrel acid he had gotten from a chemist at MIT named My Favorite Martian. I studied the tiny orange cylindrical pellet, wondering how something so small could be as powerful as they said. Mike told me that one hit of Orange Barrel carried enough punch for four good trips, so we each ate half of the four-way hit.

Shortly after we dropped it, two cops appeared and shook us down, making an extra effort to thoroughly search my wallet, but I came up clean. I worried about Mike, but for some reason they didn't go through his wallet. When they finished harassing us, they told us to clear out. Once free, Mike showed me a hidden pocket he had made under the embroidery sewn on the seams of his jeans.

The shakedown left us feeling insecure, so we drove back to Mike's apartment as the acid came on, first rising in a giddy flurry of colors, patterns, and sensations, like bubbles in a pot beginning to boil, then bubbling over into a chaotic rush of thoughts, feelings, and emotions shot through with feelings of certainty and uncertainty. By the time we got to his apartment, I had lost the line between reality and hallucination, and my mind spun in a whirlwind of kaleidoscopic madness that rocketed me back and forth through alternating fits of terror and amazement.

We found one of Mike's roommates sitting in the living room with his girlfriend. As my trip intensified toward a fevered pitch known as "peaking," Danny, Mike's roommate, seemed to be the source of all its insanity. Lanky, with long black hair and a goatee, he sat on the couch breaking open bricks of marijuana with a switch blade and weighing it out into smaller bags while his exotic girlfriend, April, watched him with dark, sultry eyes.

I felt both giddy and out of control as the acid bubbled over into a rapid-fire projection of mental events that made minutes feel like eternities. I didn't know anything that happened in that time, except that everything exploded quickly and chaotically throughout my brain. I couldn't string any sense of meaning into Danny's words, but no matter what he said, it sent me into fits of laughter, which annoyed him. He gestured at me with his stiletto while he spoke, then he turned into a huge monkey that masturbated frantically with the stiletto that transformed into his penis. Beautiful exotic April turned simian too while the two of them went through an endless series of bizarre gestures and vocalizations that sounded like screeching monkeys.

I think he threatened me with his knife, but I could only respond by laughing, thinking that he couldn't be serious. The more frantic he seemed, the harder I laughed until I couldn't stand it anymore and hurried off to the bathroom, where tiles spun around by themselves. When I looked at myself in the mirror, my face melted into a cross between The Wolfman and Mr. Hyde. The spinning continued until I couldn't find the door, then I stumbled out into the hall, turning to avoid the living room and finding myself in the kitchen, where I confronted a poster of some kind of stew that looked like the entrails of my eviscerated stomach.

Eventually the madness subsided, Danny and his girlfriend disappeared, and I went back to Mike's room, where the two of us rode out the rest of our trip. We stayed awake well into daylight, then went out for coffee, cigarettes, and breakfast. I spent the rest of that next day spaced-out in psychic shell shock, trying to make sense out of what had happened that night. Nothing I had tried—not pot, drinking, or sniffing glue—packed the punch of LSD, and nothing terrified or intrigued me more.

I never saw Danny again after that night, but Mike told me later that a couple of years prior to our meeting, four kids had thrown another kid off of a bridge, into the path of an oncoming train, killing him. One of those kids had been Danny. To this day I will never know if Danny had been serious about stabbing me or if it was in my imagination. The only thing I do know for sure is that the stiletto was real.

SIXTEEN

Slipping into Darkness

o began my passionate obsession with LSD, something that, in spite of the unprecedented fear I often experienced under its influence, inexplicably drew me to its mysteries with an all-consuming fascination that took over my life. On my second acid trip, I passed through the psychological experience of dying to the point of becoming convinced of its reality. I felt death taking me as I watched swimming colored patterns in the grain of a piece of plywood in a trance-like state, feeling my life draining away, leading me into a night full of strange sights. When I came out of the woods, a car's headlights shone on me head on, highlighting millions of floating, multicolored, sparkling, crystalline, paisley-like patterns that danced through the air, overwhelming my vision. When cars drove by me, they stretched way out, then snapped back to normal size as they passed.

My girlfriend had a job babysitting that night, so my friend Wayne and I paid her a short visit. Later, very much disoriented, we found our way back to the house around one in the morning. An angry balding man with a towel wrapped around his waist and a half-shaven face confronted us at the door, asking us in a threatening manner if we had been in his house that night.

Wayne and I looked at each other and honestly couldn't remember if we had been there. Puzzled over our predicament, we kept asking each other if we had been there. The man must have thought we were being wise guys, but in truth we found ourselves at a genuine loss to remember if we had been to his house. He ran us off, telling us never to come back.

We obliged.

My girlfriend broke up with me a few days after that and shut me out completely. I never understood it until I found out twenty-five years later that someone else had stolen booze from the man's house that night. My girlfriend's father had been convinced that I did it and told her never to see me again.

I took frequent rides to Dorchester, scoring hundred lots of four-way LSD to bring back to my small-town friends, which gave me plenty of reasons to go to school. I paid ninety dollars for a hundred hits, which I sold in a matter of days for two dollars a hit, doubling my money while scoring ten free hits for myself.

Every hit looked tiny, and the smaller the hits, the more power they seemed to pack. We tried Purple Microdot, Blue Cheer, Orange Sunshine, and lots of blotter acid, like Mr. Natural, Green Frog, Mickey Mouse, and others, then came Windowpane, which looked like tiny green plastic pyramids. All of them packed a wallop.

I soon learned that our systems build a fast-rising tolerance to LSD, making it impossible to get addicted to it. If you take a hit one day and take the same amount the following day, hardly anything happens. If you want to get a similar effect the day after an acid trip you have to double or quadruple the dose. The way to get the maximum benefit is to trip every other day, taking a day off in between to let your system recharge. It's a wonderful built-in control that allows your rational mind time to process and assimilate the experience.

I did acid every other night for months on end, running the gamut of hallucinations from fantastic magical patterns and images to terrifying, hellish phantasmagoric apparitions and landscapes. Serpentine archetypes appeared frequently. Hordes of rattlesnakes came out of holes to attack me, sending me jumping and running while larger pythons and anacondas slid across huge boulders. All kinds of them hung from the trees. No matter what kind of strange and otherworldly things I experienced, I never had any religious, spiritual, or mystical experiences, and I never considered the possibility or entertained any thought of them. I always tripped for the thrill and adventure of exploration.

In one of our government's classic cases of lies and misinformation, we had been told that LSD damages your chromosomes. For years I believed the absurdity that a child conceived at the peak of an intense LSD experience would be born retarded. This "wisdom" gave us one of our first, "profound revelations" which brought us laughter to no end.

"LSD fucks up your chromosome damage."

"Too much of anything good is bad" constituted another revelation that carried the utmost profundity.

I had the time of my life during most of my acid trips and gained many new ways to look at the people and the world around me, and I had many dark, frightening moments, the worst of them being a total bummer that rattled me good.

We decided to go to a high school dance and agreed ahead of time to drop our acid by ourselves around six and meet up at the dance, only no one else dropped at six except me. My mom let me borrow her car, which I took to the dance and parked in the lot. I went into the dance while the acid came on strong, then two cops came in, walked straight to me, and took me by both arms, escorting me out of the dance. I had about a dozen hits of acid on me, some other substances, and a few joints, and I thought the end had come.

The cops marched me out to my mom's car, where we found my dope-smoking friend from down the street in the back seat with my case of beer and his girlfriend. I couldn't believe my eyes. He hadn't even asked if he could sit in the car, let alone drink my beer, which I had hidden. Now his ignorance had me busted while peaking on acid. The cops shone their flashlight into my eyes, sending multitudes of fluctuating colored patterns and lifelike moving objects through my perceptions, while asking me what I had to say about the beer in my car.

I don't know how I kept my cool, but I did, saying, "I don't know what you're talking about. I have no idea where that beer came from. I never saw it before. I was in the dance minding my own business, and when I come out, I find you here breaking into my car with a case of beer. For all I know you put it there. Do you have a search warrant?

They seemed confused and at a loss about what to do. "Look, as far as I'm concerned," I added, "that beer came out of nowhere. I never saw it before and I don't know anything about it. Take it. You can have it for all I care. It's yours."

Being the predictable asshole cops that they were, they went for the bribe, taking the beer and telling me to get lost. As soon as they left, I high-tailed it out of the parking lot in my mom's car with my buddy Wayne, my mind bubbling over into full-blown paranoia. A couple of miles down the road, I pulled the car over and told him to drive. A mile or so later, everything seemed wrong, so I said, "What are you doing? Pull over. I should be driving."

Nothing in my world felt right. I kept vacillating between ordering him to drive, then ordering him to stop. Then I'd change my mind again because I needed to drive. Finally we parked and I escaped from the responsibility of the car, only to see all the trees melting into dark blobs accompanied by a constant low-level thumping hum that sounded like a slowly approaching helicopter. The world closed in on me, melting down and coming to an end, and all I could do was ride it out and wait for the terror to pass. It took weeks before I mustered up the courage to try it again, but try it again I did because I had survived the horror and couldn't resist the overwhelming attraction that the power and the fear held.

SEVENTEEN

Darkness, Death, and the Descending Warrior

Before long most of my small-town friends and I had huge acid parties in the sand pits about a quarter of a mile into the woods from our housing development. More than a dozen of us spent all night tripping together under the pretenses of slumber parties for the girls and campouts for the guys.

One summer night, Terry, Wayne, and a couple of other friends, and I drove to Castle Island in South Boston, the site of an old five-sided stone fort where Edgar Allen Poe had been stationed while serving in the army. A true to life grisly incident about a man getting walled up behind bricks at the fort had been Poe's inspiration for "The Cask of Amontillado." I had always marveled at the boarded-up fort while growing up in Dorchester, but I had never seen the inside. We found the fort open, so we went inside to explore under the influence of LSD, stumbling through dead-end tomb-like stone passages and doorways until they opened into empty space. Strange noises terrified us until we came across a bunch of winos who populated the place. Finding them in dark corners—babbling, incoherent, and loaded to the gills—made them seem like mythical, semi-conscious ghosts of the eerie past, which added immensely to the thrill of our acid-fueled experience.

While I lived through my small-town high school drug-and-alcohol adventures, my older sister's life continued sinking deeper into a hell that I didn't know the full extent of until many years later. I had been told that Jo Jo worked on an offshore oil rig while he was doing time in Walpole. Now my sister lived in Quincy with him, fresh out of prison, along with his twisted, sadistic mother. While my sister was pregnant with their second child, Jo Jo decided to teach my sister how to ride his full-dressed Harley Davidson Electra Glide. The bike weighed too much and she dropped it, breaking her leg, bringing still more abuse from him. He beat her, threw her down a flight of stairs, and kicked her in the stomach. My youngest niece came into the world with a deformed arm half the length of a normal one with no thumb, a weak heart, and numerous other health problems.

Jo Jo made my sister cut off contact with her friends and family, telling her he would kill her if she didn't do what he said. She had no reason not to believe him, as he had beaten and stabbed her in the arm to make his point. Over time, and unknown to the rest of the family, he beat and molested my nieces too. My mother had her suspicions about Jo Jo, but I had no idea and the girls' terror kept them quiet. If I had known, I think I might have killed him.

Unaware of the full extent of their horror, I continued my explorations that had started with alcohol, glue, marijuana, and LSD. Now I branched out with most of my friends, trying speed in the form of Mini-Whites, Black Beauties, Crystal Meth, Dexedrine, and Yellow Jackets, along with downers including Reds, Yellows, Seconal, Tuonal, Quaaludes, and other barbiturates. I never cared much for downers and thought they made you stupid, but I had to live up to my resolution of trying everything at least once.

I gravitated toward amphetamines called Mini-Whites or White Crossroads because of the lines that made a cross on top of them so they could be broken into smaller doses. For twenty dollars a hundred,

I could pop Mini-Whites and stay up for quite awhile. Utilizing my newfound resource, I skipped school as much as possible, then begged my teachers for extra assignments and would go on three-day speed runs, working nonstop to get all the work done, earning passing grades that carried me all the way to graduation.

The first time I tried crystal meth I fell in with some speed freaks and gave myself the biggest rush of my life when my "friends" slipped the needle into my arm and booted me up to the sound of Jimi Hendrix playing "Fire." The ensuing rush overpowered me, making my knees buckle. That one bang kept me up for close to three days, making me feel superhuman until I started to crash.

I went through the cycle and shot up crystal meth again and again, soon realizing that my euphoria carried a hefty price when I crashed on the down side of it. I also sensed the high doses of speed changing my personality, bringing out more darkness and paranoia. I didn't like the idea of something outside of me having that much power over me, especially when it drew me down into the darkness, so I weaned myself from it over the course of a few weeks.

Through my experiences I started to see that some substances expanded my awareness, while others contracted and deadened it. Speed gave a false sense of expansion by pumping up my metabolism and the speed of my thinking until its effects diminished, then contraction and dissolution came, not to mention the physical discomfort that the crashes brought. LSD had an expansive and wondrous effect, leaving me puzzling and questioning the accepted worldview of consensual reality, while downers and alcohol blotted everything out.

Wayne developed a drinking and downer problem that spiraled out of control after he went home one night to find his mother dead with a plastic bag over her head. She had been dead for a couple of days and her skin had turned blue. I have no doubt that she smelled bad too. After that, Wayne drank himself into a stupor all the time until he lost control one night and kept starting fights. We tried to contain him, but he wouldn't stop, and at one point he almost caused us to have an accident. Somebody came up with the idea of knocking him out, thinking it the only way to make him stop.

After a number of punches that broke his jaw, blackened his eye, and cracked his cheek, he still wouldn't go out. One of his eyes took on a vacant look that gazed off in another direction. I came to think of this as his "possessed" look because from that night on, every time he drank he deteriorated to the point of taking on that spooky one-eyed gaze that stared off into God knows where.

I couldn't take beating him anymore that first night, especially since he wouldn't go out, so I wrestled him down in the back of the car, sliding around in blood and puke until I pinned him. Then we took him back to my house, where I wrestled him into bed. He woke up the next morning—beaten, bruised, and blood-caked—with no memory of anything that happened.

When I graduated high school, most of the kids in my senior class received cars, big sums of money, or some other lavish gift. I received twenty bucks from my mom, which meant more to me than all their gifts combined because twenty bucks pushed the limits of what she could afford. At seventeen I felt anxious to get out of the house and become independent so I could pull my own weight and ease my mother's burden, and I couldn't wait to escape living with Jim, his laziness, and his ignorance.

In my senior year, I fell in love with a girl named Cathy from Maine. She had come to a party by a pond with a big, bullying drunk who mistreated her. As the night went on, his bullying wore on me to the point that I couldn't stand it anymore. I enlisted my buddy Frank to help me out with this big mouth who both outweighed me and stood a foot or so taller than me. Like I had learned from Arnie in the fourth grade, I had Frank get down on his hands and knees behind the bully, close to the embankment of the pond. I slammed him hard in the chest with my palms, sending him flying down the embankment into the water, then I stole his date and my romance with Cathy began.

By this time I had grown past being a bully myself and saw the cowardice that made bullies. It made me crazy and I couldn't stand to sit by and witness it. When I found out that a guy I knew slapped my other friend Cathy across the face, I dragged him out of a car and punched him in the face repeatedly, making sure he never touched her again. On another occasion a guy named Peter, one of the mellowest, most peaceful people I knew, became a target for another bully because he was skinny and wore glasses. I arrived at a party one night and found this jerk threatening him. I could see Peter's fear, so I confronted the bully, saying "Come on, tough guy. Pick on me. Pete doesn't want to fight you, but I will. Let's go. You want to fuck with him? You can fuck with me."

He didn't.

I had a frightening realization when Wayne met a new girlfriend and had problems with her old boyfriend. One night while I was driving Wayne's GTO, a car pulled up behind me, tailgating me and nearly running me off the road. It turned out to be the former boyfriend trying to terrorize Wayne. He came to a party later that night and my rage took over, causing me to drag him out of his car by the shirt and punch him out. All I remember is seeing red as I beat him into the ground. Out of nowhere I flew into the air the same way I had when my mom pulled me away from my buddy Paul all those years ago. Clarity returned when I saw my buddy Steve, a known brawler himself, holding me in the air, telling me, "He's had enough. You beat him and if you keep it up, you're really going to hurt him."

I will always be thankful to Steve because I had gone off the deep end. As it turned out, I had broken the kid's cheek in a couple of places and cracked his jaw. When I heard this a few days later, I felt horrified because I didn't think myself capable of doing that much damage. I never meant to hurt him that badly. I only wanted to beat the shit out of him and teach him a lesson.

I hated bullies, but I had become a bully's bully.

EIGHTEEN

From the Frying Pan into the Fire

y the time my senior year drew to a close, I had my name on the ceiling of all three cells in the small-town police station where we lived. Every cop in town knew me, and if anything happened anywhere near me, they hassled me. I knew that if I stuck around I would end up in jail, yet in spite of all my run-ins and bullshit arrests, they hadn't been able to make anything stick. I still had no record, but I knew if things continued the way they had, it wouldn't last.

I had no money for college and the Viet-Nam War continued. I feared the draft and had no prospects for self-sufficiency except factory work a few towns away. I worked in one on second shift after school. The thought of a career as a factory worker painted a bleak, mind-numbing future that I couldn't accept. Aside from that, I hated the system, but I knew I couldn't escape it, so I decided to throw myself into it. Wayne and I took military aptitude tests and scored high in electronics and mechanics, so we both enlisted in the air force in May of 1973 in a delayed enlistment program. I enlisted when I was seventeen but would ship out less than two months after turning eighteen. The doctors hassled me at my induction physical for my flat feet, telling me they would let me in if I got a note from my family doctor, so I went to him and said, "Hey, Doc, I need a note from you for the air force."

He said, "Do you want to get in or get out?"

"In."

"No problem."

I had to hustle all the way up to the last day of my senior year, and ironically the grade I needed to pass came from wood shop. I hurried to finish my project at the very end of that last day, barely passing with a C-, and by miracle of miracles, I graduated high school. After graduation I took a dirty, mindless job in another factory for more money to tide me over, comforting myself with the fact that it was temporary. Soon afterward my brother got his girlfriend pregnant, so my friends and I partied like wild men when my first nephew came into the world, smoking pot and drinking all afternoon and into the night until we passed out in the wee hours of the morning. We woke up a few hours later to a breakfast of two or three different kinds of speed chopped up and mixed together. We snorted the burning concoction and followed it up with a couple of shots of whiskey. While my brother started his new family, I made plans for basic training and my schooling in electronics. I planned to send for my girlfriend Cathy to come with me, marry me, and be my partner in my grand adventure.

On a cold day in January, a week after the holidays, I left my twelve-year-old little sister behind along with small-town life, Dorchester, and Massachusetts. I barely slept after an anguished last night with Cathy, the love of my life, but the call to escape drove me out of there to explore a bigger world that could not be denied. I left home for air force basic training, carrying a small denim duffel bag with one change of clothes and a couple of science fiction novels my mother gave me. She drove me to the induction center in Providence, Rhode Island, where they handed me my plane ticket and orders. Then she took me to the airport. Wanting to numb the ache of leaving Cathy and my mother, I persuaded my mother to let me buy her a drink. She rarely drank, but when she did, she liked scotch, so I ordered a scotch-and-water for her and a rum-and-Coke for me. We had a couple of drinks, so I felt pretty good boarding the plane, but the numbness from the alcohol couldn't dull the pain from an unexpected lump that rose in my throat when I said goodbye to my mom while she cried softly. Once on the plane, I continued drinking rum-and-Cokes, saving the little rum bottles they called nips. I knew I wouldn't see alcohol or anything else for quite some time, so I drank all I could.

The shock of my drastic change of lifestyle began soon after landing in San Antonio, where basic training inducted me into a harsh new reality. Drill instructors lined us up and barked at us while hustling us onto buses. I had a hard time taking them seriously in my intoxicated state and it was all I could do to keep from laughing out loud. My fellow enlistees had flown in from all over the country, coming in every color and accent; some scared, some indifferent, and some, I'm sure, drunk like me.

Once we were on base, they continued barking and lining us up, putting us through our in-processing. They made a big deal out of the fact that my mother's birthday didn't appear on any of my forms. I told them that she wouldn't give it to me and that they were welcome to ask her themselves. That seemed to satisfy them. They kept at us until two thirty in the morning, finally assigning us to a two-story concrete barracks, where I fell into my bunk, drunk and exhausted.

I discovered sleep deprivation to be the first part of their attempted brainwashing when they woke us rudely a short while later at five o'clock to drive us through one of the longest, most painful days of my life. I came out of the black hole of unconsciousness still drunk with the beginnings of a major head-banging hangover creeping into my brain. They marched us down to the chow hall, where we felt like outcasts. They called us "rainbows" because we still had multicolored civilian clothes and long hair. Everyone else had shaved heads and green fatigues. We spent the whole day marching around, first getting issued four hundred dollars advance pay in cash, then to get our heads shaved. Following our shearing, they issued us fatigues, khakis, dress blues, shoes, combat boots, and underwear. Prior to 1974, the air force only issued boxer shorts. I made my mark in history by being one of the first to be issued briefs.

As the hours passed, my headache came on with a vengeance along with the growing horror that my life would be hell for the next six weeks, maybe longer. That afternoon they took us to the base exchange to purchase razors, blades, combs, shaving cream, and other articles paid for out of our four hundred dollars. By the end of the day, we had full-issue, including duffel bags, and we looked like all the other recruits at Lackland Air Force Base.

They confiscated all of our personal items, including rings, watches, and my rum bottle collection. Then they kept at us until nine o'clock that night, wearing us down and leaving me with a headache that felt like a railroad spike driven into my skull. I collapsed into my bunk and fell fast asleep until I was awakened again at five the next morning. My headache had finally gone, but my attitude became less than enthusiastic, so I started thinking about escape plans, wondering how far I would get with my government-issue haircut and green clothes.

They taught us many useful skills, like making a tight military cornered bed, how to fold our underwear in thirds to exactly the length of a dollar bill; how to spit-shine our shoes, clean the nozzle of our shaving cream can and toothpaste tube with a cotton swab so it looked perfect, precisely align our insignia on our dress blues, and space our uniforms evenly on the rack. Inspections came regularly, and if things didn't look perfect, the whole rack of clothes ended up strewn across the floor. It was the same with our security drawer, which had to be perfectly covered with a towel with all our toiletries laid out clean and orderly. If anything looked out of line there, they threw it and all of its contents across the floor.

I hated all of it.

We had to run a quarter of a mile that first week; a half a mile the second, working up to a mile and a half the last week, which had to be done within a certain time. I decided to quit smoking my two and a half packs of Marlboros a day when I nearly vomited the first time I ran the quarter mile, but that only lasted a few days because our drill instructors made us stay in formation for long periods of time, unless they said, "Smoke 'em if you got 'em," which made smoking the only way to get out of formation.

A small, scrawny guy named Strand from New York who wore big glasses had the bunk beside me. Though he was skittish and afraid, I liked him and took him under my wing. I'm glad I did, because Strand needed me when a tall black guy named Holmes who stood behind us in formation got into the habit of making fun of and threatening him.

I knew Strand wouldn't say anything to our drill instructors, because he didn't want any trouble. Holmes kept giving him a hard time about being a "cartoon-character-looking motherfucker," and poor, terrified Strand didn't respond, which only made Holmes come on stronger. Finally I had enough, so I turned around and said, "Why don't you shut the fuck up and pick on someone your own size, Holmes? If you can't do that, pick on me."

"You probably came from some upper-middle-class white family, didn't you?" he said.

I sensed that he knew the opposite to be true. As it turned out, he came from a well-off family and nobody liked him, not even the other blacks. I studied him, ready to go for it, but he backed down, barely managing to save face. He didn't hassle Strand anymore after that.

Aside from pulling KP, everyone caught dorm guard duty that rotated through the squadron. Each of us had to do a four-hour shift day or night, whenever it came. If you pulled it during the night, you lost out on four hours of sleep. One morning we awoke at the usual time, only it seemed very dark. Halfway through making our beds and preparing for inspection, someone saw by their watch that we had actually arisen at two in the morning instead of five. It didn't take long to figure out that Holmes had been on dorm guard and decided that he wanted his sleep, so he turned all the clocks ahead three hours to skip out of it. Everyone really hated him after that.

As each week of basic training passed, we gained incremental freedoms that showed us that there might be light at the end of the tunnel. Our dorm consisted of two big rooms with two rows of ten bunks in each row, with our lockers lining the walls. I don't remember how it started, but when things had relaxed somewhere in the middle of basic training, a pillow fight erupted between our side of the dorm and the other. Having extensive experience battling my brother, I went deep into the other dorm, beating and chasing away anyone who came near. Someone gave me a shot to the side of the head that bounced me off the wall, but it didn't slow me until someone yelled, "Hold it. Someone's bleeding. There's blood on my pillow."

We stopped and looked at our pillows, then a few other guys noticed blood on theirs too. We couldn't figure it out until someone pointed to me. I reached up and felt a wet spot in my hair, but I didn't care. I didn't feel any pain and I sure as hell didn't want to stop the pillow fight. I had been having the time of my life!

Later that night, while watching television in the dayroom, I ran my tongue up to my upper molar on the side of my head that had hit the wall and it crumbled into three pieces. The base dentist put a temporary cap on it and instructed me to have it fixed after I arrived at my permanent duty station.

I realized much later that I scared people with my insane ferocity, which cemented my connection and respect with the black guys in my squadron along with the fact that they hated Holmes for being an asshole too, and I had put him in his place. I found myself developing the same kind of friendship based on mutual respect that I had with my black buddy Bruce from junior high and my black friends Marcel and Willie from Boston Tech. In truth I didn't feel much connection with the white guys in my squadron because most of them did come from upper-middle-class families while the black guys came from poor families like mine. In spite of all the racism and prejudice I had experienced and contributed to, I had more in common with the black guys, especially one named Johnson, a cool cat whom I saw as the ringleader.

We marched a long distance one day in ninety-plus-degree heat and returned to air-conditioned barracks, where I caught a chill. When awakened in the middle of the night for dorm guard, I felt zoned-out and disconnected as if engulfed in a strange fog. I don't know how I finished my duty, but I did, then I crawled back into bed. When they woke us a few hours later, I couldn't get out of my bunk.

I felt covered in lead when I dragged myself to sick call. As soon as they looked at me, they sent me to the hospital in an ambulance, where I spent four days drifting in and out of consciousness. It felt like something out of a bad horror movie with them waking me every four hours to take blood. The whole time there, I had to listen to another recruit who cried all the time after getting a tracheotomy. When I came back from the haze, they told me I had both German measles and pneumonia.

My favorite drill instructor told me that though I had missed the better part of the last week of basic training. It consisted mostly of tests and I had shown enough aptitude for him to waive them and let me graduate with the rest of my flight. On the Saturday afternoon, at the end of basic training, when everyone else came back from their one-day furlough in San Antonio, I came back from the hospital, weak but functioning.

On our last night before shipping out to tech school, my black buddy Johnson flabbergasted me when he asked me if I remembered how to roll a joint. "I have a buddy who's been stationed here permanently," he said, producing a small bag of pot and some rolling papers.

I felt honored.

He had the rest of the black guys surround us and keep a look out while I rolled a couple of good-sized joints behind a towel. Then just like I had done with Willie and Marcel; Johnson, one other black guy, and I slipped off to the parade field and enjoyed our first high in a month and a half.

I felt a great thrill being stoned under their noses in the middle of a military basic-training facility where they supposedly had your mind and body under their control, and I felt thankful to Johnson for choosing me over a lot of others as one of the people to share his weed with.

NINETEEN

Learning the Hard Way

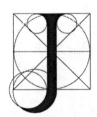 ohnson and I both went to Keesler Air Force Base in Mississippi for tech school, but we ended up in two different squadrons. Soon after arriving I got a Dear John letter from Cathy, which broke my heart, so I drank excessively whenever I could to numb the pain, often drinking through the night until sunrise.

At Keesler I took an eighteen-week self-paced basic electronic development course called BED, followed by eighteen weeks in Electronic Warfare Systems Specialist School. The first part of BED focused on algebra and I fell into a rut struggling over capacitive and inductive reactance along with other formulas and subsequently failed my first major test. After studying and retesting, I scored higher but still failed. I thought I had washed out, but they assigned me a tutor, and on the third try I passed.

Once past the math hurdle, I flew through the rest of electronic theory, finishing the course seven weeks ahead of schedule with a high average. My drive to absorb everything I could about electronics and the concepts of energy and its behavior gave me the foundation for my understanding of reality. Oscillators, resonance, tuning, harmonics, resistance, inductance, waves, transmitters, receivers, negative and positive poles all taught me the nature of energetic manifestations. My electronic training catalyzed my understanding that ultimately there is no distinction between matter and energy; only a difference in its form. I understood matter and energy as one and the same thing.

While engrossed in school, my buddy Bob, a red-haired kid from Ohio who roomed across the hall from me in the barracks, told me we could get all the speed we wanted free and legally by breaking open Vick's inhalers and swallowing the inner part because it contained Dexedrine. We did this, and sure enough, we got high for a couple of days, but it made me sick to my stomach, and I belched menthol the whole time. For years after that, every time I smelled menthol I became sick to my stomach.

One morning before sunrise I spotted a plastic bag on the path in front of the chow hall. I picked it up and looked inside, finding marijuana. I looked around and didn't see anyone, so I pocketed the weed, ate at the chow hall, went to school, then tracked Bob down as soon as I could.

We bought some rolling papers and I rolled a joint, but no place on base felt safe, so we headed for a small wooded lot not far from one of the base gates. Finding a hidden spot behind some trees, we lit the joint and took a hit. No sooner had we done this when a new recruit in fatigues came out from behind a log as if he had been lying there waiting. "Hey," he said, coming on strong. "I'd really like to buy some of that. I'll pay whatever you want. How much can you sell me?"

Being startled by his sudden appearance and insistence on buying pot, combined with the fact that he had busted us cold, put my radar into high imminent-danger mode. I handed him the joint, saying, "This is all I have, but I'm more than happy to share it with you."

Mild surprise passed over his face. He took the joint, took a hit or two, then said, "That's all I need. I have to get back to my barracks."

As soon as he disappeared, Bob and I did the same. Both of us felt spooked. We went back to our barracks, goofed off for a little bit, and did some studying before going to bed. I left the pot in my pants pocket, which I put in my locker.

My roommate, Mike, was a Mormon from Wyoming full of a "golly, gee whiz" innocence and naiveté that I both pitied and envied. His worst curse word summed up the extent of his jaded life with the expletive "bullroar!" He and I made quite a contrast between my short stature and his tall, square-jawed studiousness and Clark Kent eyeglasses. They called us the odd couple.

Our first sergeant shocked the two of us when he burst into our room with the security police late that night searching for pot after Bob and I had been caught by the suspicious recruit. They started going through all of our clothes and personal things while I stood there in my underwear, so I announced that I wanted to put my pants on. No one said anything, so I put on the pants I had been wearing with the pot still in the pocket.

They went through everything I had except the pants I had on. I saw poor "golly, gee whiz" Mike terrified out of his mind. Bob and I kept exchanging nervous glances across the hall when no one else saw us. Finally they closed the door and said, "No one leave their rooms. We're bringing the dogs through next."

I climbed back into bed, under the covers with my pants on. When things grew quiet, I pulled the covers up over my head, pulled out the half ounce bag of pot and started eating it, plastic and all, but I couldn't swallow because my mouth was too dry, so I thought, the Hell with it. I'm going to the bathroom. I slipped out of bed, then crept down the hall, half expecting some cop or dog to spring out of the shadows, but all remained quiet. I spit the pot and plastic out of my mouth and emptied the rest of the bag into the toilet and flushed. They brought the dogs through the next day while we were in school, but they never found any pot.

While I continued getting educated in military tech school, my sister's husband Jo Jo blessed everyone by dying from a cerebral hemorrhage after abusing my sister for seven years, leaving her damaged along with my two nieces. I found out that in my absence, after getting out of prison, Jo Jo had gone to my mom's house and had a confrontation with Jim, eventually pulling a knife on him. My poor mom had had surgery the day before, but she still managed to get between them and break it up. My sister called her soon afterward, crying in terror, so no one ever pressed charges.

I'll never know if I would have followed through, but a fantasy had been forming in my mind to go home on leave, buy a stolen shotgun, and blow Jo Jo off of his full-dressed Harley, but he did us all a great favor by dying. I didn't go to his funeral, but I heard that his biker friends went into church, surrounded his coffin, and each drank a shot of tequila in his honor. One of them stole the church's microphone. They all wore cutoff denim vests "flying their colors" with big embroidered patches on their backs that said FTW.

My grandmother asked my sister what FTW meant and my sister told her "flowers, trees, and woods," but it really stood for "fuck the world." The bikers drove out to Jo Jo's gravesite in formation and passed the tequila bottle around, drinking more shots in his honor before smashing the empty bottle on his coffin.

No one can ever say that Jo Jo didn't go out with a bang, only most of us wished it had come sooner.

TWENTY

My Dark Mentor Appears

I left Mississippi in October of 1974 trained as an electronic warfare systems specialist, heading for my first duty station at an air force base in the Midwest, where I would be surrounded by mile after mile of cows and corn. I discovered that most of the guys stationed there shared my passion for smoking pot, drinking, and doing drugs. With the Viet-Nam War still going on, many of them had recently returned from Thailand with wild tales of the black market, easy-to-procure drugs, and beautiful women for the equivalent of five bucks a night. At my first opportunity, I put in a "dream sheet" and volunteered for duty in Thailand.

With plenty of drugs and partying going on around me, I fell into the familiar groove of selling illicit substances, which had become second nature for me. I considered drug dealing a step up because nobody had to lose out from the theft that precluded the sale. Instead everybody gained from the products that were bought and sold. I had done more than my share of bad things, but I didn't think of myself as bad in my heart, and I had never been convicted of anything. As I moved semi-consciously into incremental increases in self-awareness, I felt the battle raging inside of me intensifying between what I thought of as good and evil. In my life to date, I'd had no strong male role models I could respect, so I walked with my feet in both worlds, thinking that I had no one but myself to teach me anything.

It's been said that the teacher appears when the student is ready. In my case I must have been readying myself for a bigger dance with darkness, because a mentor soon appeared who would school me in the darker realities of a life of crime outside the honor among thieves that I had grown up with in Dorchester.

After breaking the facial bones of a few guys I had fought with, I worried about my problem with violence and excessive force. I wanted to learn how to cause maximum pain and minimal damage. Two guys who lived beside me in the barracks had studied kung fu in Thailand and offered to work out with a few of us and give us free lessons.

Unfortunately my teachers didn't have long before their enlistments ended, and when that time came, we had a big celebration that took us to a strip club across the street from the base where we drank pitcher after pitcher of beer until the table overflowed with empties. When it came time to leave, I stood and started for the door with the rest of the gang. As I walked past the table, I heard glass breaking behind me. I looked back to see what caused it and saw nothing. When I turned forward again, a fist slammed into my chest, knocking me to the floor. I struggled to get back on my feet, slipping all over the beer-covered floor while chaos broke out around me. Another mystery foot found my chest, sending me sprawling to the floor again. Then everyone ran for the door because the cops had been called. I could hear the approaching sirens. I scrambled to my feet and headed after them. Glancing back, I saw a short, muscular, wild-looking man with long red hair and a goatee standing amid the confusion. I realized that he had been in the middle of the fight.

Once outside, I saw the cops approaching, so I sprinted for my van and pulled up to the front of the bar, where I picked up my friends, one of whom had been beaten. I drove away moments before the cops pulled in behind us. When everything blew over, we saw that nobody had been seriously injured, so we went to a Denny's restaurant to join the bar-closing crowds for breakfast. When we walked in the door, my breath caught when I saw the wild-looking red-haired man, and I braced myself for a fight. This time I would see it coming instead of getting sucker punched, but to my amazement, he came over and greeted us.

Dan, whom I had never seen before, had been the bouncer at the bar and turned out to be a good friend of my karate teachers. He joined us for breakfast and apologized to me, explaining that the guy who he had beaten walked out behind me and smashed a beer mug into the table of mugs and pitchers. When Dan heard glasses breaking, he thought I did it because he couldn't see the guy who broke them behind me. When I heard the breaking glass, I looked back and not only didn't see Dan's punch coming when I turned forward, but I never saw who hit me.

A few days later, when visiting friends who lived off base, I came out the door and saw Dan, who, as it turned out, only lived a few houses away. I asked him if he wanted to smoke a joint and he agreed, cementing our friendship. In a short period of time, we dropped acid and took other drugs, spending many a wild night in every kind of bar imaginable.

"Dirty Dan," as he liked to call himself, fascinated me to no end. He seemed like every kid I had grown up with in Dorchester rolled into one. With his long red hair, goatee, and piercing ice-blue eyes, he often twisted his moustache with a maniacal look, claiming to be Satan; and he looked like it, especially when we dropped acid. Ten years older than me, Dan understood the streets on a far deeper level than I did. He had done a total of eight years of hard time in San Quentin, Folsom, and Soledad prisons in California and had recently been paroled to the Midwest, where he lived with his sister and her husband, a tech sergeant in my squadron. At the time I met him, Dan attended college, majoring in psychology.

He told me he had murdered two people, one a friend who planned to testify against him and his friends in a drug trial. They drowned him by holding him under water on a waterskiing outing. As Dan explained it, the prison sentence for murder in California carried a shorter term than the sentence for drug trafficking, so by killing the snitch they came out ahead whether caught or not.

I'll never forget his response when I asked him how it felt to kill someone like that. He looked me straight in the eye, answering from the depths of a hardened, cold-blue gaze that protected his pain, saying, "You live with it."

Dan had also shanked a guy in the joint, fatally stabbing him with a crudely fashioned prison knife. In prison he joined the Aryan Brotherhood, which meant he had joined for life, making him both protected by and beholden to them. If someone in the brotherhood had problems with someone outside of it, another member far removed from the conflict would get the order to kill the offender for their brother. Dan's turn had come and he delivered.

Because of our mutual trust and "honor among thieves," Dan took it upon himself to school me in the ways of life and crime. He taught me how to set up a successful drug operation, the finer points of intimidating people, and how to use a knife effectively for attack and defense. I had carried a knife for most of my life in Dorchester, but I learned from Dan that I knew almost nothing about using it right.

Throughout our intense relationship, we took turns dragging each other into dangerous situations. I look back on many of them with shame and regret, but I realize that Dan instigated and perpetrated the shameful one, and easily lured me into them because we both knew that no matter what happened, each of us would be there to back the other one up. I understood this as a Dorchester rule: honor among thieves and backing up your partners, a way and a code of life that we both lived by, creating a strong bond of loyalty that held us together.

We tested it often.

TWENTY-ONE

Satan Laughs at Me and I Have a Narrow Escape

iring of the constant shakedowns at the base gates, I thought hard about living off base. Dan helped me make my decision when he married a doe-eyed, innocent young girl named Nancy after getting her pregnant. We rented a big three-bedroom house on the north side of town with another friend. Dan found a job pumping gas, which surprised me until he concocted a plan for me to come take all the money from the cash register. He planned to hit himself with something, then call the cops to report that some black guys robbed him. Fortunately he got fired before he could put his plan into action.

We constantly worked on angles to set up crimes, but Dan took a bolder approach. His spontaneity made him much more of an opportunist. I had my "morals" and kept my thefts to institutions and businesses. I stole more for the thrill than anything else and I ended up giving most of what

I stole away, but Dan had no boundaries when it came to theft. Anyone and anything could be fair game. This never sat right with me, but he knew my weaknesses, and his opportunism drew me into a few reluctant heists because of my own fear and misplaced loyalty.

Anything could happen when we went out. One night when I drank too much, he talked me into grabbing a woman's purse from a chair in a bar. I hated purse snatchers and thought of them as the lowest form of life, but in my drunkenness, Dan convinced me that this wasn't a snatch. Like a puppet, I did what he said and some guy came at me from the bar, yelling about me stealing the purse.

Dan came out of nowhere, punching the guy in the face, knocking him to the floor, and accusing the would-be hero of stealing the purse. Then he grabbed the purse and gave it back to its owner, acting the part of the hero while I slunk out the door, relieved that it didn't happen and ashamed that I had tried.

On another night he talked me into following a couple of women home to their apartment. He listened at the door while they talked and decided to go out again. Once they left, he broke the front door open and helped himself to their stereo, jewelry, and some other items. He gave me the stereo, but I never felt good about it and felt relieved when I finally got rid of it. He woke me up another night, coming to the door with a car full of a television, a stereo, jewelry, and a wad of money, telling me he had met a woman in a bar and went home and slept with her. After they had sex, she fell asleep and he took everything of value he could find, hauling it all away with her car.

During this dark, chaotic time I dreamed about playing music for a living, thinking that music made people positive and happy and that it would be a good purpose for my life. My father had been a drummer and I had played on two snare drums in my bedroom during my teenage years. The drums seemed like they could provide the path I needed. Somehow a jam session came together at our house between my pseudo-musical friends. People brought lots of instruments, setting them up in our cellar. No one really knew how to play, so after making some noise, everyone drifted off. Some guy brought a drum set that he left behind for a couple of weeks.

I came home from work one day and Dan told me the guy had finally shown up looking for his trap set. Dan told him that he hadn't seen any drums since the jam session a couple of weeks ago and that he was welcome to look through the house all he wanted. The drums had never left the cellar, where the guy had originally set them up. He looked downstairs, but according to Dan, he didn't see them. Dan told me that the guy's attitude and actions, combined with the way he had left the drums for two weeks, convinced him that they were stolen, especially after the guy gave up on them so easily. After telling me the story, Dan said, "Take the drums. They're yours, but you'd better get them out of here in case the guy comes back."

I took them to a music store and traded them in as down payment on a brand new five-piece set of stainless steel Ludwig drums and a set of Zildjian cymbals, then I started taking drumming lessons in earnest. When I went home on leave to Massachusetts and proudly set up my shiny new drums in my mother's basement, she shocked and mortified me when she said in all seriousness, "They're really nice, honey. You'll be able to get good money if you have to hock them." Up to this point, I hadn't known that my father hocked his drums on a regular basis when he needed money. In her mind she was thinking practically.

The house we shared became a major party house until it became too much for poor innocent Nancy. She and Dan soon moved out to a trailer closer to the base. I had fallen into a routine of taking my bong out every day soon after waking and hitting my way through a book of matches, taking twenty hits of good Columbian reefer before rolling up a few joints to take to work.

In spite of the military's chicken shit, I liked working on aircraft and solving electronic problems, especially when stoned. After my twenty-bong-hit breakfast, I went to work and met my friends for a midmorning break to smoke a joint or two. Then we went to someone's room in the barracks for lunch, stuffing a towel under the door to keep the smoke in and opening the windows for marathon smoking sessions. In the late afternoon, we slipped off again for a few more joints, then I went home to my bong.

On days when I didn't have to work, I went to the freezer for a cornucopia of choices for the day's libations, among them LSD, cocaine, amphetamines, downers, and hashish. We liked experimenting, so we shot up LSD, which felt like flipping a switch and instantly tripping.

Shooting cocaine gave me a powerful rush that seemed to end by blasting out through the pores of my nose.

During the summer a gang of us went to a huge pond somewhere out in the corn fields, where we swam and partied all day and night. While partying there I made friends with a long-haired, fun-loving crazy guy with a mischievous glint in his eye, whom we called Madman Tim. Tim turned me on to my first hit of angel dust, otherwise known as PCP.

I took one hit from a bong and the PCP overwhelmed me while continuing to come on even stronger until I didn't think I could take any more. It kept coming. Terrified, I ran out to Tim's front porch and vomited, thinking I was dying. I heard maniacal laughter amid my violent retching and felt sure that the mocking voice of the devil laughed at me as if he owned me, reveling in my sickness, waiting for me to die so he could snatch my soul. I held on for dear life until the terror and sickening sensation abated.

In spite of my initial terror, I had another opportunity to smoke it some months later. Once more, I got sick and vomited, but this time the devil wasn't laughing at my seeming brush with death. After my second try, I decided that smoking angel dust wasn't for me. On my home front, things deteriorated to the point that our living room stayed full of people partying or sleeping twenty-four hours a day, waiting for me when I awoke in the morning, and waiting for me when I came home from work, remaining there when I went to bed.

One day a black guy who worked as an administrative assistant in our squadron told me that he had seen paperwork coming across his desk stating that the cops were preparing to raid our house because of the traffic that passed through there. I went home and spent the whole night packing everything I had into my van. I pulled away as the sun rose. I drove to a friend's house and asked if I could sleep on the couch until I figured out what to do.

The cops raided the house a few weeks later and busted the people who had made themselves a home in the living room. They netted a small cache of drugs, but nothing of any great quantity. I berated myself a thousand times over for being so stupid, at the same time being thankful that I had been warned. I took a few weeks' leave to lay low in Massachusetts and let the trouble pass.

TWENTY-TWO

A Moving Target with a Guardian Angel Makes Love to a Witch

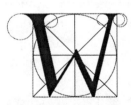hile home on leave in Massachusetts, I saw that after the horror of Jo Jo my sister had reconnected with her first love, my buddy John's older brother Tony. It brought me great joy to see my sister's life coming back together after so much darkness.

My father went to prison when I was seven and my younger sister never really knew him. I saw him once after he got out at his father's funeral when I was fourteen. He had located my older sister shortly before I went home on leave and invited her, Tony, and me to dinner in Boston's Chinatown. I felt a little shocked at how small and frail Mickey looked to me now that I had grown. At five foot three, he stood hunched over from his war wounds, and he walked with a limp from the shrapnel in his hip. He talked fast and his eyes darted everywhere, no doubt watching for someone he owed or had ripped off. The four of us ate Chinese food and kept ordering beers after dinner. Mickey went to the bathroom just before the check came. We knew he expected us to pay for it, but since he had invited us, we kept drinking until he figured out that we didn't intend to pay, then he hustled us out of the restaurant. On our way to a bar, he ducked into an alley with us, obviously avoiding somebody.

Once at the bar, he introduced my big sister first as a hooker, then as his daughter, but I could see that no one believed anything he said. When we parted ways later that night, I lied about where I had been stationed, as I feared he might try to take financial advantage of me. My sister, Tony, and I continued partying until dawn. Then Tony and I dropped my sister off and went to a diner for breakfast before I dropped him off. It turned out to be the last time I ever saw Tony and my father.

I returned to the Midwest more aware and wiser from the close call I'd had before leaving, but I still had much to learn. Jim, a soft-spoken air force buddy from Oregon with black curly hair who had connections, invited me to move in with him. Aside from our mutual interest in drugs, Jim had a proposition he had worked out with a group of shady bouncers from the bars he liked to hang out in. During World War II, before the United States had such ridiculous hemp laws it paid Midwest farmers to grow cannabis for its hemp. A lot of plants still grew between the corn fields, but they had no intoxicating qualities. Jim's bouncer buddies wanted us to work with them sneaking through corn fields doing all night pot harvests for thirty dollars a pound. They planned to ship it to Texas, where a chemist would treat it with angel dust to be sold somewhere else. Jim bought a new van and we spent many all-nighters packed into it like storm troopers, skulking through cornfields, sometimes getting eerily spooked by the wild cries of coyote packs, the fear of shotgun-toting farmers, or the appearance of a county sheriff's cruiser.

I didn't like one of the bouncers who came off as a big bully, so I brought Dan around to see how tough this big mouth really was. As it turned out, two of the other bouncers had been in county jail with Dan in California and were terrified of him, which balanced things out for me. After a while, I just didn't like the scene anymore and started drifting away from it. Soon afterward the cops arrested Jim with a bunch of the non-intoxicating hemp plants and confiscated his van while bringing him a slew of legal hassles. Once more, like the glue bust, house bust, and other close calls, spirit guided and protected me through my madness.

My dream sheet came through and I received orders to Thailand. I couldn't wait to escape from the Midwest. Somewhere in that same timeframe the cops busted a friend of mine from Philly. They found some of my stash in his freezer, but he didn't give me up. I felt bad when it happened, but I understood that he brought it on himself.

One of Jim's bouncer friends had a connection for the amphetamines we called Mini-Whites and I soon ended up strung out on them, staying up for days straight until I became hallucinatory and dissociative to the point of thinking that my friends wanted to jump me. While it was at its peak and I was driving in my van, I turned a corner and forgot where I had been going or what I was doing. I barely even knew who I was. In the midst of this craziness, I got mixed up with a girl called Flash who claimed to be a witch. She had been with a few of the other guys before and found her way to me. Sexually aggressive, I found myself living an amphetamine-fueled sexual fantasy with her until it came down around me one night when we fell into an exhausted sleep, nude, in the back of my van on a dirt road, somewhere out in the corn fields.

A couple of county cops rattled us awake with their flashlights on our bare bodies. The cops looked through my things while asking me questions. I picked up a quarter pound bag of marijuana and held it right in front of them, saying, "Nothing here." One of them found my triple beam scale and asked me if I was a reloader. I had no idea what a reloader was, but I said yes.

Spirit was definitely watching over me that night, because the cops had me cold, but by some divine blessing they missed everything! My van had become stuck in the dirt on an embankment and the cops planned to tow it. I pleaded with them and they gave me eight hours to get it out of there. I went to the base and found a friend with a four-wheeler and a winch who pulled it out for me, then snuck Flash into the barracks and went to sleep.

The CQ (charge of quarters) found us and gave me a hard time, but he never escalated it or told anybody else. I ended my tryst with

Flash, whom I realized brought bad energy, and resolved to make this mindless adventure the last time I let myself get strung out on amphetamines. That same morning I had to pee in a cup to test for drugs as a prerequisite for shipping out to Thailand.

The irony is that I didn't get caught doing amphetamines. A week or two before the test, I had been partying at the pond. I drank a lot one night and stumbled across one of my friends eating a pile of wet white powder from his hand. I asked him what he had and he said it was Phenobarbital that he forgot he had in his pocket. It had dissolved while he swam, so he wanted to eat it or lose it. He offered me a bitter pile, which I accepted. When I woke up the next morning, I forgot I had taken the Phenobarbital and it showed up in my urine sample. The air force canceled my orders, sent me to talk to the shrinks, and put me in a program people called "golden flow," during which they randomly called me to pee in a cup twelve times in thirty months.

I resented this to no end.

I had a lot of anger inside of me and hated the system more than ever, but I still struggled to come to terms with it. In fits of childish resentment, I broke and threw away the coffee cups of my supervisors and anybody else who gave me trouble. I also wrote a stack of obscene statements that I put in their personnel files. The battle raging inside of me intensified and I felt jerked back and forth between opposing energies that felt light and dark. In spite of the bad things I had done, I still felt like my heart had not gone bad at the core, yet I felt compelled to rebel against the system in every way I could think of. No matter what they said or did, they weren't going to own me.

I spent a short time in the golden flow program and had a historical moment when then President Gerry Ford came to our base. While I was on my way in to pee in a cup, his motorcade drove by, so I waved at the stretch limo and Gerry spotted me, giving me a big wave back. It struck me as ironic that I was waving to the president while on my way to a drug test. When I went in to test, they had someone watch me pee, which I thought of as humiliating. I managed to squirt hand soap into my urine sample when they weren't looking, which made them call me back again because the sample had been spoiled. The next time I took a plastic bag and cut the corner off of it, then I attached a thin plastic hose to it with silicone sealant. I plugged the end with a sawed off pencil tip, filled it with Budweiser, and strapped the rig to my chest, running the tube down so it would be ready and waiting at my zipper. When this test came back they called me in to talk to the shrinks again, who informed me that my tests kept coming back adulterated.

I told them that it wasn't my fault that they couldn't do anything right. Additionally I said I had grown tired of their harassment because they kept calling me in for tests that they kept screwing up and it wasn't right that they kept hassling me for their own incompetence. Finally one of the shrinks asked me what I wanted. I said that I wanted them to quit hassling me because I had a year and a half to go before my discharge. If they left me alone, I would do my time quietly and take my hard-earned honorable discharge with all my benefits. They agreed and I managed to escape their scrutiny, but I still had volumes to learn.

TWENTY-THREE

I Hit Bottom

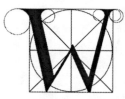ith all the drug busts that happened to my friends and my own continued close calls, I became more vigilant, but I had a lot more than cops to worry about. I became aware of events that happened every year around April when they stationed new people at our base. More often than not, attractive girls appeared, and with their presence the party activity increased. I learned from Dan to keep my cards close to my chest and only deal with people I knew well. His advice paid off because soon after the new party people arrived, they disappeared and drug busts came out of nowhere, causing me extra worry about people getting busted who might rat me out.

As time passed, my worry came from a short, husky guy named Ben who lived in another barracks. Ben supposedly had good connections and a reputation for knowing karate, which made everyone afraid of him. I gave him some money for drugs and he strung me along for weeks, never delivering, but I kept my cool and continued trying to connect with him. I wasn't sure how to handle the situation until he took some money from one of my good friends and did the same thing to him, which set me off. I might have let things ride with Ben as far as I was concerned, but to do to my friend what he did to me felt worse and proved to me that he had no intention of giving me the drugs or the money he owed me.

I found out when he would be in his barracks and confronted him in a crowd of guys, asking for both my money and my friend's. Ben gave me the same run around that he had given me all along, so I punched him in the face. I'll never forget his shocked and fearful expression when I knocked him on his ass in front of all those people. My one punch destroyed his ego worse than any physical damage I might have done, and he crumpled so easily it spooked me.

He didn't come back at me either. He said that it wasn't fair because I had sucker punched him, but I had hit him straight on. He made a big show of going to the gym and fighting fair with me, so I did, beating him repeatedly in one of the saddest, most pathetic exchanges I ever took part in. He came at me three times, and three times I took him, but I didn't punch him out, because he lost so easily. Instead I wrestled him to the ground and pinned him. He finally gave up after his third defeat. I had our money a couple of days later. After that lots of people went after Ben. He had been ripping people off for some time, and everyone feared him because of his supposed karate expertise until I took him down in front of a crowd, opening the door for everyone else. A few months later I heard that he got busted.

I went to the chow hall one day and saw him eating lunch with a guard for an escort. He said "hi" and acted friendly. I said "hi" back and slipped out the door, putting distance between us fast. Who knows what he may have said, but they had to catch me in the act of selling to someone or catch me with the goods to bust me. So far I had been able to avoid both of those situations.

While I passed through these adventures, Dan had adventures of his own. He and poor naive Nancy, who turned out to be his second wife, had their child, and their ill-fated marriage dissolved. After his divorce, Dan wasted no time looking for his third wife. We started hanging around with Cindy and Lou Anne, a couple of girls I was stationed with. I never thought Dan would go with Lou Anne, as she didn't strike me as attractive, but he did and they soon married. She got orders to a base in Northern California near where Dan came from and they would soon be leaving, but not before Dan pulled a couple of more capers.

We went out drinking one cold, bitter winter night and ended up at the bar of a Holiday Inn. Dan latched onto a harmless good old boy having the time of his life in the "big city." The poor farmer didn't have a mean bone in his body and had simply been out for a good time with no bad intentions. After he spent a couple of weeks attending a veterinary school that taught him how to artificially inseminate his cows, this Saturday gave him his last night out before going back to his farm life, and he had been drinking heavily.

When closing time came, Dan asked him if he wanted to come with us and meet some girls. We took him to visit Cindy and Lou Anne for a while, then headed back for the hotel, only Dan had me take another route, telling me to drive us out to a corn field. To my surprise, Dan took out a gun and threatened this poor drunken farmer, who begged and bawled for his life. I couldn't believe what was happening, but my misguided loyalty wouldn't let me betray my partner. Besides, he had the gun.

Dan took all the guy's money, his wallet, and his keys. Realizing that I had become an accomplice, I started calling Dan Lefty and he called me Butch. Dan had the poor guy take off his clothes and lay face first in the middle of a corn field in the cold, telling him, "I'll be watching you from a distance. If you move I'll kill you."

I felt the deepest shame I'd ever felt in my life over what happened. I would have felt different if the guy had been a bully who deserved humbling, but this hillbilly's biggest crime constituted getting drunk and wanting to meet some girls. He didn't deserve this. We drove off, leaving him in the cold, and went back to the hotel. Dan asked me to help him go through the guy's room, but I wanted no part of it, so I left him there. He took everything the guy had, including his car, and went on a spending spree for the next few days with the guy's credit cards. The whole thing felt like a nightmare. Every time Dan showed or offered me something of the guy's, I declined.

Not long after that dark night, Dan asked me for a ride. It being the middle of the day, I thought I was taking him on an errand until he went to the door of a house and broke it in, helping himself to a load of camera equipment and a stereo. I couldn't leave him there, so I waited, once more becoming an unwitting and unwilling accomplice. Once more, I refused any share of the loot.

Dan and Lou Anne left for California soon after that.

TWENTY-FOUR

A Cosmic Flash

he lesson I learned from the bust at our house and from what Dan taught me showed me that people coming there drew attention, not only from the cops but from other people who could cause trouble. I wanted to do things differently and avoid problems, but as careful as I played it, problems still arose in ways I couldn't have imagined. Dan told me that to sell drugs successfully, I had to keep myself isolated by not letting anyone but a few trusted associates know where I lived, and he said to deliver the drugs to those who wanted them so the traffic coming to me didn't make me the center of the activity. I only gave my contacts my phone number. I had developed a good relationship with a gangly, dark-haired dealer with dark, sunken eyes and a droopy moustache named Terry who managed four apartments in an old converted mansion. For tenants he had a couple of sweet little old ladies who always baked cookies and cakes, which gave us a perfect front. I

rented an upstairs apartment. Any big drug exchanges we made went through the inner hallway and up the stairs from his place to mine, so no one saw any traffic between us. I kept the attention off of myself by driving different routes so I didn't establish any patterns. Hardly anyone knew where I lived and my stash and money stayed safe.

Terry had connections for many interesting substances and he introduced me to some new experiences, but he had a weakness for downers, which caused problems that I didn't anticipate. I had learned my lesson from being strung out on amphetamines, but I still hadn't woken up enough to see the quagmire that threatened us from Terry's developing problems. He had access to diabetic hypodermics and liked to shoot things up, and some of what he offered provided experiences that I had yet to try. So far I had shot up crystal methadrine, LSD, and cocaine. With Terry I tried heroin and PCP.

I didn't have any satanic experiences when I shot up angel dust. Instead I felt very drunk, like I was floating through a fog. Everything moved in slow motion, as if I lived in the bottom of a huge barrel of Jell-O. Heroin put me way down under in a different way. Thank God its energy didn't appeal to me. I felt drawn to LSD and other more visionary experiences.

In parallel to my growing relationship to Terry, I developed a solid friendship with a guy in my squadron from East St. Louis. Stocky, with brown hair and a moustache, Killer Miller turned out to be one of the best friends I ever had. After my talk with the air force shrinks, I had an offer to work the graveyard shift, which meant seeing less people and less contact with the military, which I couldn't wait to escape from. Killer and I both worked graveyard and usually went back to his house in the mornings. When his wife went to work, we went to bed, with me sleeping on the couch. We slept until the afternoon, then each drank a six pack of Miller beer, smoked lots of weed, and worked on our vans.

While I was finishing the last year of my hitch in the air force, my brother moved to Southern California. I went out to spend a couple of weeks with him, and for the first time in my life, I was exposed to peace, love, and the concept of being a vegetarian, which made sense to me at the time. My new "hippie" perspective intensified the battle raging inside of me between what I thought of as good and evil. With Dan no longer there to drag me down into the darkness, I thought there might be hope for me to be a good person. With all I had been through, especially with Dan, I still didn't feel as if I had gone bad in my heart.

After visiting California I settled into a groove working graveyard shift, issuing electronic components and sleeping in the back room because things moved very slowly. Outside of work I ran my drug business, making deliveries and pickups and having fun keeping things low key, until someone tried to set me up at a party at Killer's house. A friend of his had a girlfriend whose father was a chief of police. She came to the party with a guy that none of us knew and disappeared a short while later, leaving her friend behind. After a little time passed, he asked me if I knew where he could buy some drugs. I said no. Then to Killer and some others I said, "Does anyone know this guy?"

No one answered. Then I said, "How did you get in here and who are you, that you come to a party where no one knows you and ask people if you can buy drugs? You a cop or something?"

He made lame excuses and disappeared in a hurry. Feeling spooked, I took off after he did, half expecting a full-on raid. I hid my stash and laid low for a few days, telling Killer that his buddy's girlfriend had tried to set us up. He agreed and cut her loose.

In my quest for new experiences, I felt driven to try everything I could; the more illicit the better. Having seen so many lies and hypocrisy from our government, I hated the system more than ever and figured that if they made it illegal, it had to be good. I had no real awareness of it at the time, but my hunger for new experiences spearheaded my search for purpose and the meaning that had been lacking in my life. I had done all manner of mind-altering substances, but I never had anything remotely resembling a mystical or religious experience, unless being laughed at by the devil while I thought I was dying could be considered mystical. I never thought of it that way. I thought of it as a paranoid drug episode.

On June 21, 1976, the day of the summer solstice, at the age of twenty-one, I had a profound mystical experience that transformed me to the core of my being and changed my life's direction forever. The battle between the energies inside of me that I thought of as good and evil had reached a fevered pitch, flip-flopping back and forth endlessly during the course of a day, driven by the fury of my frustrated anger.

Both good and bad, Terry had procured many novel substances for me that I had yet to experience, among them Hawaiian baby woodrose seeds, a species similar to morning glory, classified as Argyreia nervosa. Woodrose has the distinction of being the most potent of this class of hallucinogens, with lysergic acid amide concentrations up to three times that of other morning glory species. LSD-25 is d-lysergic acid diethylamide. Baby woodrose doesn't contain diethylamide, but its lysergic acid amides are still psychoactive.

I didn't know any of this at the time. I only knew that the woodrose came from a plant and taking it supposedly had similarities to LSD, my favorite drug, so the idea of taking something new that occurred naturally in a plant appealed to me, particularly in light of the fact that I had become a vegetarian.

I chewed thirteen rosewood seeds on an empty stomach on that warm summer day and drove out to the swimming pond to party with my friends. There the rosewood seeds came on strong, building steam, but never with any edginess like the frenetic energy of LSD. I ended up alone, floating in the middle of the pond on a big truck inner-tube under warm sunlight. In that magical moment, my flip-flopping rage peaked and my perceptions opened like unfolding blossoms. My whole being expanded, making me highly aware of the magic, complexity, and connectedness of everything both through me and in me. All the while the struggle of light and dark raged insanely inside of me. I had too many contradictions in everything I thought, said, and did.

In a cosmic flash, all of the pieces snapped into place. I looked to the shoreline and saw the exact point where the water met the shore; where the earth and water touched, warmed by the sun and cooled by a gentle breeze, meaning that all of the elements—earth, air, fire, and water—became present at that exact moment, making it the meeting point and center of the universe. In that same flash, I had the realization that in truth I constituted the center of the universe. All of this and more instantaneously flooded me in abstract symbols and archetypal images that communicated information faster, better, and more condensed than any language ever spoken.

In the infinite variety of life experiences that we share with others, none of us truly knows each other's thoughts. We may have psychic, telepathic, and intuitive flashes, but in the end all we really know and all we really have are our own thoughts that drift and scatter into strange places when we lose consciousness, fall into sleep, or experience any number of shifts in our awareness. We receive life through five senses where sensory impressions come to us at our center. We are the focal point where everything comes together, hopefully making sense to us in a meaningful way. If we cease to exist on this earth, it is a two-way street. Not only do we cease to exist on this earth, but the earth also ceases to exist for us and the rules of stimulus and response change.

How could the earth possibly exist if there were nobody there to perceive it?

II

SPROUT

TWENTY-FIVE

Bottom Feeders

neffable defines what words are inadequate in trying to describe. It is something packed so densely with information, emotion, and meaning that your mind is forced to wrestle with abstractions to bring reason to a non-rational experience that ultimately makes greater sense than anything the rational mind could comprehend. Because of its nature, much is lost in my feeble attempt to put what I now think of as the cosmic flash into words, so I can only hope that its power and intensity are at least glimpsed by my description.

I had literally seen the light, and knew I had to make drastic changes in my life to resolve the glaring contradictions that made up who I thought I was. I felt like I had awakened in the middle of an uncomfortable dream where I had fallen deep into a complex web of relationships with drug dealers and buyers who expected certain things from me. I couldn't suddenly change directions without freaking a lot of people out. I had to move slowly and deliberately to extract myself from the quagmire I had created. I had structured my life around illegal activities because that was all I ever knew. In my mind, most cops, politicians, big business, and figures of authority had less integrity than common criminals because they hid behind the symbols and trappings of their stations to commit even bigger crimes against more people. Society looked down on the Mafia, but I saw no difference between them and big business or politics. Where could I find ethics and integrity in so much madness?

With little more than a year and a half to go before my discharge, I resolved to cut my illicit ties in the Midwest and move to California, where I could start a new life. Meanwhile I would continue my drug experimentation, especially in light of my life-changing revelation, and when my year and a half came to an end, I would disappear.

I embarked on a two-year plan to wean myself from taking anything that altered my consciousness so I could remove all external influences from my perceptions and try to make sense out of reality with a clear mind and body. As part of my plan, I decided to purify myself by becoming a vegetarian and fasting to clean out the toxins I had been taking for most of my life. I fasted two and a half days every week beginning Saturday night and ending on Tuesday afternoon for the greater part of my last year and a half in the military. Though I was on a new, self-chosen path, no one in my life knew of the radical inner shift I had experienced. They continued with the way things had been, unaware of how different my thinking had become and of how much I wanted to change.

Above all, I still wanted to try everything possible in hopes of finding something that affected me as profoundly as the woodrose, until the opportunity came for me to try a new, wholesome, unadulterated life in California. I had my whole spiritual path neatly worked out, but reality turned out to be far messier than I planned. Terry's dark side and weakness for downers brought me into contact with people and experiences I would have avoided. I had become deeply involved in drug business with him and I lived in the apartments he managed, so I found myself caught in the inertia of what we created while the force of its momentum swept me further into the darkness.

My plan had gone smoothly until a few months before my scheduled discharge from the air force, when Terry became involved with a loser with rotting teeth, bad breath, and long, dishwater-colored greasy hair who called himself Fast Eddie. Terry invited me to a party one night at his place and I found myself caught up with a gang of scumbags. In my conflicted state, I took a Quaalude Terry gave me and drank a number of beers, which zoned me out far worse than I anticipated.

I don't remember much of that night, but at some point I pissed off Fast Eddie and he smashed an empty pint rum bottle over my head. I didn't feel anything when he did it, so I didn't even realize I got hit. Sometime later I made my way back upstairs to my apartment and passed out; waking up the next day to a head that felt sore and tender.

I saw Terry later that day, and to my horror he told me I had pissed off Fast Eddie, who said I had promised to sell him some cast aluminum "brass" knuckles I had. It sounded like bullshit to me, but having barely any memory of the previous night, I couldn't refute it, so I told Terry I didn't remember saying that and I didn't want to sell the knuckles. I only had a few months to go before my discharge, and I wanted nothing more than to disappear from the Midwest and reinvent myself in California. I discovered that leaving what I had created wasn't going to be easy.

I still worked the graveyard shift with Killer Miller and bought a dirt bike that I rode to work. When I came home, I went to bed around seven thirty every morning and slept until early afternoon. Now that I had the dirt bike, I parked my van at Killer Miller's and began putting a new engine in it, upgrading it from a six-cylinder to a beefed-up V-8 in preparation for my trip to California.

I awoke one morning, roused from a deep sleep by a knock on my door. Wearing only my underwear, I crawled out of bed asking who it was. Terry answered, saying he needed to talk to me, so I opened the door to let him in and he came flying forcefully into the room, followed by Fast Eddie and two of his buddies. One of them stood by the door and one of them blocked me while I stood there, vulnerable in only my underwear. Eddie threw Terry up against the wall and pistol-whipped him across the head and face with a .45, demanding forty bucks that Terry supposedly owed him.

I had a shotgun in the closet along with five pounds of marijuana and a stash of other drugs, but I would never make it to the closet with one guy on me, the other covering the door, and Eddie up in Terry's face with the gun. Even if I made it and had a gun battle with them, I was history because the cops would bust me, not only for whatever became of the shooting but for all the illegal substances I possessed.

Terry begged me for the money, so I gave up the forty bucks and Eddie and his buddies left, leaving Terry beaten and bleeding. I watched them from the window as they left, thinking that I should blast them right then and there with my shotgun. Then I thought, *Life is worth more than forty bucks, and if I shoot them here, the cops will come and I'll go down for it, drugs and all. Forty bucks isn't worth it.*

I was furious at Terry, not only for bringing them to my door but also for not telling me he had someone with him when he knocked, but they had him at gunpoint. I also knew that our cover was blown. These lowlifes would march in whenever they wanted to extort money, and we were helpless because any retaliatory action on our part would bring them to our door, and any confrontation there would bring the law, who would shake us down and find our drugs.

Terry changed after the pistol-whipping. He wanted to save face, which had been lost, and I have no doubt that the depth of his involvement with the downers muddied his thinking even further. A few days after Eddie's visit, Terry showed me a small .32 semi-automatic pistol he had purchased illicitly. He talked big with it and flashed it around, letting me know that he wouldn't be taken advantage of again.

About a month before my discharge, I had another rude awakening while asleep in my apartment late one Saturday night when I heard a key slide into the lock of my front door. I looked at the clock: two in the morning. I thought about going for my gun, but I knew Terry, being the apartment manager, had the only other key, so I crept to my bedroom door in the darkness and watched as he entered, carrying a shotgun and talking incoherently to himself. I didn't want to make any noise for fear of startling him, so I remained quiet and watched as he went to the front room and stationed himself by a window, gun at the ready.

This is too weird, I thought. *He let himself in without knocking, so he doesn't think I'm here, and he's talking to himself, not making any sense. I'd better disappear for a while.* I faded back into the darkness, gathered some warm clothes, and slipped out the back window into the freezing night. I couldn't get to my van, because I had parked it under the window where Terry waited with the shotgun, so I walked a few blocks in the bitter cold to a friend's house and rang the doorbell, apologizing for waking them, then asking if I could crash there for the night. They let me in and gave me a spot on their couch, where I eventually drifted off to sleep.

I awoke to the sound of a radio. Then I heard a news flash about a man who had been gunned down in the middle of the street. When I heard the address, I knew it was Terry.

TWENTY-SIX

Another Glimpse of Light before Darkness Rushes in Again

I made some phone calls and found out that Terry had gone to a party the night before and got into a fight with his wife. When another friend stepped in to calm them down, Terry pulled out his pistol and waved it in the guy's face. I knew the guy. He was a loyal friend, but Terry's fear had gotten the best of him, causing him to threaten this recent returnee from Viet-Nam.

In her anger, Terry's wife had gone home with the friend who had tried to help. Terry went back to his apartment, where he grabbed his shotgun and waited for trouble from the upstairs window of my apartment. The night passed without trouble, so Terry stormed back to the other guy's place that morning to get his wife. When he barged into the other guy's house, the Viet-Nam vet waited for him, sitting up on the back of his couch with his rifle at the ready. He shot Terry once through the neck before Terry turned and ran for the street. Then he shot Terry twice more through the back, dropping him in the middle of the street, collapsing one of his lungs. The paramedics rushed Terry to the hospital, saving him. After Terry got shot, Eddie and his moron friends thought I was gunning for them. I'm glad they thought I was coming, but in reality, gunning for them was the furthest thing from my mind. I planned to be discharged from the service and free from the madness in a month. All I wanted was to get out of town and start my life over again in California, the way I had planned for so many months.

I figured that the cops would be crawling all over the apartments, and I didn't want to go anywhere near there for fear of getting busted, so I decided to disappear until things blew over. Killer Miller lived on the other side of town, so I went there to lay low. A few nights later, when things felt calm, I went back to my apartment, cleared all my things out, and faded into the night, never to return. I spent my last few weeks in the air force staying with Killer, finishing my out processing. After my discharge I planned to head for California. Shootouts and lowlife scumbags didn't fit into my new worldview.

Killer and I fell into a routine of going to work at midnight, then heading back to his place in the morning to smoke a little weed and drink a few beers before going to bed. We'd wake up in the afternoon and work on our vans until dark, then party when his wife came home from work before we had to go back at midnight for the late shift. While sleeping on his couch one day, I had another experience that had a major impact on my life when I awoke one morning from a vivid, nearly lucid dream. I opened my eyes to see Killer sitting in a big stuffed chair at the end of the couch by my feet. I couldn't contain my excitement and started telling him my dream.

"I came into awareness on the flight line, working on the underside of an aircraft in a fuel cell packed with electronic gear. I looked down at the ground and saw it moving. Then I realized that the jet was taking off with me in it. The ground moved faster until we became airborne. Then we started an ever-steepening climb that brought us perpendicular to the ground, heading straight up, accelerating faster and faster with each passing moment. The electronics around me turned into cockpit controls and I found myself hurtling toward the sky in a space capsule that shot to an unimaginable height before falling back toward the earth. The ground flew up at me as I plummeted, swallowed by both gravity and terror. At the last possible moment, I stopped inches from the ground, floating. No space capsule. Only me. Floating. My experience felt as lucid and concrete as real life until I woke up to see you sitting there."

He smiled and his eyes twinkled after I told him my dream. "Do you remember the red switch above you in the capsule that you pulled?"

"Red switch? I never said anything about a red switch…" How would he know whether there was a red switch? I suddenly remembered seeing a red switch in my dream capsule and pulling it, making the capsule go down. I hadn't remembered that detail of the dream until just now when he told me about it. "How did you know?"

"I hope you don't get mad at me," he said, "but I've been telling you what to dream for months now."

I couldn't believe what I was hearing.

Killer leaned back in his chair, saying, "During all these nights that you have been sleeping on my couch, you've been talking in your sleep until I came in one night and held a conversation with you while you slept. I did it with my brother for years, so it seemed natural to do with you." He paused and studied me for a moment, letting his words sink in. "If you want to know the truth, I've been taking you on dream adventures for over a year, telling you what to dream. This morning I came into the room from behind you and you said, 'I'm glad you're here. I've been expecting you,' before I came anywhere near you or your line of sight. I acknowledged you and sat down in this chair and we talked. You stayed in an open, hypnotic-like state, ready to create the realities in your mind that I told you to create."

Many of my conceptions about the nature of reality shattered that day in a most exquisite way. Boundaries and limits I had held from my life's experience dissolved and unlimited possibilities bubbled forth.

My discharge was scheduled for January 6, exactly four years since I had enlisted, so I spent most of December with Killer and his wife, keeping a low profile, getting ready to leave town. As soon as I out-processed, I planned to head straight for California. We had a party a few days before Christmas. In the middle of it, I received a phone call from my brother in California who told me that Tony, my sister's first love, whom she had reunited with, had been depressed and went to a vacant lot where he stuck a rifle in his mouth and blew his brains out. My mother was in Connecticut, tending to my dying grandfather, and my brother had just moved to California with his wife and two kids and didn't have any money to do anything. He had been trying to call my sister all night but didn't get an answer and feared that she might be trying to kill herself, so he said, "The ball's in your court. You're the only one in a position to do anything."

I called and let the phone ring and ring and ring, until my sister finally picked up, sounding as if she spoke from the depths of some dark subterranean cave. I told her I'd be getting out of the service in a few days and that I would come get her and the kids and we could go to California to start a new life together. All she had to do was hang tough for a few days. She did and I drove through the snow from the Midwest to Boston, where I spent a few days selling what we could of hers and setting out again for the Midwest in my van with a huge storm coming right behind us. After finishing up my military business, we took off for California.

TWENTY-SEVEN

California Dreaming

I became an instant father figure at the ripe old age of twenty-two, now responsible for my withdrawn sister and her two little girls, age three and seven; all of them victims of physical, emotional, and sexual abuse. I didn't realize the extent of their damage until we stopped for gas in New Mexico. When I pulled up to the pump, I saw that my cherub-faced oldest niece in the front passenger seat had been sitting in a puddle of urine.

"What happened?" I asked, puzzled.

She looked up at me with her big blue eyes. Her whole body shook. "I was too scared to ask you to stop."

"Why would you be scared to ask me to stop?"

"My father always wanted to make good time when he drove, and he got mad and beat me if I asked him to stop for the bathroom."

My heart melted when I heard this and I wanted to kill Jo Jo all over again. "That's not the way it is with me," I said. "If you need to go, you just ask and I'll stop for you. You don't have to go on the seat, okay?"

She nodded.

"Get yourself some clean underwear and clean clothes and get your mom to help you clean up. I'll take care of the seat. You don't ever have to do that again. Just ask and I'll stop for you."

After staying with my brother for a few weeks, we found a three-bedroom house a few blocks from the beach in Southern California and made a home using cardboard boxes for tables and some old furniture some friends of my brother gave us. The beach community my brother found turned out to be a happening place full of peace, love, vegetarians, LSD, marijuana, and other substances, shared with love. As far as I knew, no losers knocked on doors trying to extort small change from anybody, and nobody shot at anybody else.

Most Friday nights I found myself on the beach at sunset, tripping on two or three hits of LSD. The energy from the environment and the people passing through it felt palpable to me, and I thrilled myself picking up on the different energies. I discovered that no place is a total paradise and every place has a dark side one night at a party. While tripping on acid, I literally watched the good vibes flowing back and forth between people as colored energetic waves until two guys came in and the colors disappeared. It struck me as the strangest thing to see all the energy drain from the room. After a few minutes, the difference in energy made me uncomfortable, so my friend and I left. Once outside, I asked him about the two guys, as their presence had changed the energy of the whole place. When he told me they were junkies, it all made prefect sense.

At home my sister drank herself into oblivion all the time. Practically every night, she and my nieces cried out in their sleep from nightmares, usually involving Jo Jo, who still terrorized them from beyond the grave. Armed with what I had learned from my dreaming experiences with Killer Miller, I talked to my sister and the girls and worked with them and their dreams to help them overcome their fears.

My sister told me that Jo Jo hated crosses and reacted strongly when he saw them. At one point when the nightmares seemed overwhelming,

I made a cross out of sawed off broomsticks and hung it over the door, inside my niece's room. Whether psychological or "woo woo," I'll never know, but their nightmares diminished.

Encouraged by all I had learned, I worked diligently at my own dream work, recording and analyzing my dreams and the dreams of others. I reached the point that I spent forty-five minutes every morning filling six pages of a notebook with my night's dreams. I had many spiritual dreams and some truly remarkable and amazing experiences, two of which stood out above the rest.

In one I found myself outside my body roaming, around the neighborhood and the alley outside our house. It felt very real. In another I found myself in the presence of God, who manifested as brilliant white light. God informed me telepathically that I could ask and receive the answer to absolutely any question I could imagine about anything at all. That sublime moment felt more real than life itself, and in it I felt I had the complete knowledge of the infinite cosmos at my disposal. I felt so flabbergasted by the power of the experience that I couldn't think of anything to ask and the dream faded away, leaving me wide awake, full of wonder and longing.

My plan was to get a solid job to pay the bills and pursue my music career on a separate track, financed by my day job. I spent most of the year on unemployment, working at temporary electronic technician jobs and pursuing singing and drumming lessons. I practiced drumming six hours a day until I got a little notice and someone invited me to join a three-piece rock-and-roll band. We played bars, weddings, and keg parties, picking up a few bucks for our work but never getting ahead. I spent a lot of time writing songs and poetry, while rehearsing a couple of nights a week with the band.

For someone who planned to purify himself and quit all manner of self-intoxication, I found myself inundated with temptation. My bass player had an endless supply of cocaine that he always shared, and he had a solid connection for Columbian marijuana. He often fronted me pounds that I turned over, making quick money for short work. From my friends at the beach I had all the LSD I wanted and I hung out regularly in a bar, drinking on average a six pack of beer a night while smoking an ounce or two of good Columbian pot every week. I still longed to make my break from getting high so I could perceive reality with unbiased perception, but it wasn't coming easy.

To further challenge me, I heard from Dirty Dan, who lived in Northern California with Lou Anne. He pleaded with me to come visit so he could show me where he came from and introduce me to the people he had told me many stories about. Between one of my temporary jobs and a break in band practice, I packed up a healthy stash of pot, LSD, and whatever else I had, and headed north for a reunion with my dark mentor.

TWENTY-EIGHT

A Babe in the Woods

I drove north in my van and found Dan and Lou Anne living in a small house in Northern California. A day or two after I arrived, Dan and I took a road trip so he could show me his stomping grounds and introduce me to some of his "homeboys." Lou Anne had to stay behind and work, which turned out to be the best thing. We drove through the mountains, camped, and took some LSD before heading for the Sacramento area to spend some time with his cousin Steve, another crazy redhead with long stringy hair and maniacal Charlie Manson eyes who had done time in San Quentin for possession of a small amount of marijuana. The marijuana laws back in the '70s carried severe penalties compared to California's present, more enlightened laws. Steve had also done time for other crimes. When we went to visit him, he worked in a warehouse and lived with an attractive prostitute and a big dog. He acted suspiciously toward me, partially, I thought, because I was ten years younger than he and Dan. He didn't take to me until something Dan said changed his mind. I never knew what it was, but after what happened, I understand his hostility and why he acted the way he did.

We went to a biker bar full of ex-cons, hookers, and Hell's Angels, and I turned out to be the youngest among them. We had a good time drinking, shooting pool, and smoking dope while the women called me "babe," referring to my youth compared to the others. Dan wanted to see Charlie, another friend of theirs who had been in and out of the joint with them, and Steve knew where to find him, so we tracked him down. Charlie and I hit it off right away. Soft-spoken and baby-faced, he struck me as one of the mellowest and most considerate people I ever met. I soon discovered that Charlie had escaped from jail and found an unhappily married woman desperate to escape her wicked husband. Charlie killed the man and took over his identity. When I met him, Charlie had been living undetected under the other man's identity for more than two years.

In those few days that we visited, I met a number of Dan's homeboys who at that time didn't reside in prison. I knew most of them from the stories Dan told me, and they had become legends in my mind. For someone who had a dream of becoming more spiritual, I now found myself hanging out with some bad dudes. With guys like these, both loyalty and treachery ran deep, constituting an accepted and established code of behavior otherwise known as honor among thieves. Together, Dan, Steve, Charlie, Steve's hooker girlfriend, and I headed out to the mountains for a few days of camping. Once they were out in the wilderness, their inhibitions dropped and I saw reality emerge.

We went to a small mountain lodge that had pool tables and a bar and had just settled in, shooting pool and drinking beer, when Dan went to the bathroom and came out a minute later, saying with some urgency, "Come on, we're leaving."

"Let's finish our pool game first," Steve said.

"We need to leave now. Don't draw attention. Just get up and go like we're leaving normally, but we have to get out of here fast."

We piled into my van and took off, driving quickly through the mountains, putting distance between ourselves and the bar while Dan explained. "When I went into the men's room, I recognized a guy who had been a snitch in the joint, so I waited for him near the door. When he came out, I stabbed him up through the sternum, going for his heart."

I never found out if the guy lived or died.

Dan's matter-of-factness about the stabbing amazed me, even more so because of his sense of duty in dealing with a snitch who came from inside of prison, outside its walls. We found an out-of-the-way place to camp that night and all of us took a healthy dose of LSD that I provided as my contribution to the party. We had a fun-filled, playful time, and in my mind everything felt harmonious.

In retrospect, in spite of my street smarts, I played the role of a babe in the woods with these guys, and if I ever had any doubts about having divine protection, this adventure proved that it had to be working for me. I discovered the complexity of it when I awoke the next morning to find Charlie gone.

"Where did Charlie go?" I asked.

Dan shook his head. "Charlie was paranoid that Steve and I took him camping up here in the mountains to kill him because he was afraid that we thought he had been disloyal to us over something that happened in the joint."

"How will he get home?"

"I'm sure he stole a car and is long gone from here."

Dan and Steve shrugged it off and didn't seem to think much of it, so I let it drop. Years later, after pondering how Steve acted, I'm pretty sure that Charlie never made it home alive.

After dropping Steve and his girlfriend at his apartment, Dan and I drove back to his house, where he talked to Lou Anne, making plans to come live in Southern California after her discharge from the air force. I drove back south and settled into my groove of working, being an uncle, playing in the band, drinking, smoking pot, and doing drugs, still thinking and dreaming about the day I would leave my intoxications behind.

A few months later, Lou Anne received her discharge and she and Dan came south to live close to me, my sister, and her kids. With Dan once again in my life, our wild adventures continued, only now I had the responsibility of my sister and her kids, which narrowed my opportunities for trouble and kept the insanity in check. Dan and Lou

Anne struggled to make ends meet, but life with him and his chronic criminal ways brought financial challenges. I tried to help him when I could, and he repaid me when he could, in his own ways.

I had a friend who had a quantity of hashish that he wanted to move quickly and Dan said he had friends in Northern California looking for some, so I helped arrange things so Dan could take the hashish north and make some money for everyone. He took the hash north and didn't return. When I went to check his apartment, I found it vacant. Fortunately my friend knew I wasn't in on the rip-off and didn't hold me responsible, but I did feel personally responsible, as I had brought Dan in.

When Dan contacted me a few months later, I asked him what happened. He made excuses, so I told him not to bother me anymore. I had spoken for him to help him out and he ripped off my friend and betrayed our loyalty while trashing my credibility. It had been a matter of trust and my word, and he had disrespected it, so I had no more use for him in my life. My schooling with my dark mentor had come to an end, and it had come none to soon.

TWENTY-NINE

Following the Straight and Narrow

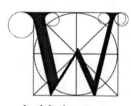ith Dan no longer a force to contend with, a big obstacle had been removed from my life. After moving to California and dealing with the trauma of my sister's life, I had slipped back into the darkness with Dan, all the while struggling to hold the intention that came from my cosmic flash. Now my path looked clearer.

I did psychic experiments with my sister and others while working actively with my dreams, occasionally getting startling results but never getting anything repeatable or consistent. I still drank, smoked pot, and did drugs, invariably ending up stoned and drunk on Saturday nights, feeling half asleep and bloated from stuffing my face. I always packed myself full, while holding a tangible emptiness that nothing could fill. As time passed, I realized that it had been more than two years since my cosmic flash. Since then I had survived even more treacherous depths than the ones I had been in when I had that first awakening.

Each time I found myself intoxicated, I reaffirmed my intention to extricate myself from the morass and chaos in the new year. I had a few months to prepare, so with an approaching self-imposed deadline, I made a plan to have one last big indulgence. I wanted to live as naturally as possible on a vegetarian diet without taking anything into my system that didn't provide nutrition, which to me meant giving up alcohol, caffeine, marijuana, drugs, aspirin, medications, and anything else I didn't think of as being part of a natural diet.

On New Year's Eve, on the threshold of 1979, when I was twenty-four years old, I took two hits of LSD, smoked a lot of cannabis, and indulged in my last high. The next morning I worked hard at getting clean and modifying my lifestyle to fit the path I envisioned. I fasted often, stuck with my vegetarian diet, and thought about other things I could do to keep myself healthy while becoming more spiritually aware. Before leaving the Midwest, I had visited a health food store and restaurant run by students of Kundalini yoga. With that memory in mind, I looked for Kundalini yoga classes in the phone book and discovered an ashram.

I threw myself into yoga, waking at four and arriving at the ashram at five for an hour-and-a-half session before getting to work at seven. After a couple of hours home for dinner at night, I went to band rehearsal until ten, while continuing private voice and drumming lessons on Saturdays and off nights. I made it to bed at eleven thirty most nights and arose at four the following mornings to start all over again. I did this for a few months until I became sick from exhaustion. I couldn't see myself giving up my dream of being a high-paid musician, especially after putting that much time, money, and lessons into it, and I had to work a full-time job to live, so I gave up yoga.

In my electronic work, I rode the wave of technology, first working on tube equipment, then transistors, followed by integrated circuits and microprocessors. Everything I learned about electronics worked in parallel with my growing understanding.

After two and a half years of living on the West Coast, my sister wanted to go back east to visit my mother. We planned to move out of the house we lived in, put our stuff in storage, and come back and find a new place. We flew back east for a couple of weeks, and when the time came to return to California, my sister informed me at the last minute that she wasn't coming. I felt saddened and empty at the loss of my nieces.

I decided to go to school using the G.I. bill. I still planned on following my music career, but I also felt a need to expand my technical career path. Jim, my drumming teacher, had recently divorced and purchased a boat. He had also given up getting high and offered to let me live on the boat with him. If I liked it I could start paying rent. I ended up staying for six and a half years, keeping most of what I had in storage with my sister's abandoned possessions. I missed my nieces in those first months and had a rough time adjusting, as much of what I had done revolved around them. Now, unexpectedly, I had my own life again and I found myself back to where I had been when I got out of the service: free, with no commitments or responsibilities except to myself.

Jim practiced a meditation he learned from a man named Roy Masters, who had a radio show called "How Your Mind Can Keep You Well." Roy had an organization called the Foundation of Human Understanding based in Los Angeles. When I first listened to him, he seemed egocentric, but the more I listened, the more I heard profound things come out of his mouth. What really appealed to me about Roy was that he sold his book, *How Your Mind Can Keep You Well*, along with three meditation tapes for twenty-five dollars. If you wrote to him and told him you couldn't afford it, he sent the book and tapes for free, no questions asked. After living on the earth for close to a quarter of a century, I finally heard a male authority figure whom I respected because he spoke and lived his truth.

What a concept.

I ordered and paid for the tapes and book and soon practiced Roy's meditation in the morning and evenings, learning how to quiet my thoughts and stay in the moment. Not only is this difficult, but I also found it impossible to continue for any length of time. I read all of Roy's books and went to see him in person numerous times, learning many things that still guide me to this day. Though I never heard him using the word *impeccable*, Roy taught me what it meant to be impeccable. He also taught me that you will become what you hate. Additionally I learned about people who drained you of time and energy. Roy called them psychic vampires. I also learned to "do what is right in your heart," which was another way of telling me to follow a path with heart. Most importantly, I learned the wisdom of the statement, "Know the truth and it will set you free."

I saw Roy lecture many times and had the honor of being the best man and sole attendee when he performed a wedding ceremony for Jim and his new wife Cindy. I saw Roy at one of his lectures and told him how many I had been to and how much I had learned. He smiled and said to me, "What are you doing here now? After all you've learned, you don't need me anymore. You have enough to move along on your own."

Had he been less than impeccable, he could have pumped up my ego and asked me to donate more money or increase my commitment to him in some other way, but he didn't.

A year after I moved on the boat, Jim moved in with Cindy, giving me the first solitude I'd had since getting out of the air force three and a half years earlier. It also gave me time to live my life for myself again. I had been clean for a couple of years, but still felt driven to push the boundaries of my experience, so I took up scuba diving. Then I bought a bigger motorcycle and tried skydiving, bungee jumping, and flying ultralight planes. Each of them gave me thrills like I had experienced as a kid climbing high into trees and jumping into the water from bridges and cliffs. I took foolish chances on my motorcycle and had a maniacal daredevil mentality that kept pushing the boundaries of fear, life, and death.

I went through a number of bands, ending up in a country western band that played regular gigs. I didn't care for the music, but I liked having a regular gig and soon slipped into one of my hyper-grooves, working full time, attending college two nights a week, and playing in the band four nights a week. I tried to stay active in the music, but I wasn't thrilled about playing country western, putting up with the drunks in the bars, and the cigarette smoke and late nights that went with it.

Things grew more difficult when the company I worked for was bought out and they wanted me to relocate. I didn't want to, so I spent a couple of months commuting long distances while playing music and attending college on the same hectic schedule. The pace ran me into the ground physically, mentally, and emotionally, but once I took the layoff and finished the semester at school, things settled down. With unemployment I had the freedom to take a breather, like I had originally planned to do after being discharged from the air force.

THIRTY

Death Revisited

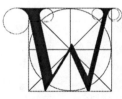ith a few years of staying clean behind me, no job, and no real responsibilities, I planned to stay out of work for as long as possible so I could pursue my spiritual path in earnest. I thought about returning to yoga, but the martial arts seemed more practical because karate moves would complement my drumming. Aside from that, I still carried a knife everywhere I went, and I wanted to learn some self-control so I wouldn't damage anyone. I hoped that the martial arts would give me the confidence to overcome my fears.

The meditation I learned from Roy Masters helped me spiritually, but I wanted to improve myself on all levels, so I signed up for a year's worth of karate lessons, attending both morning and evening classes in an effort to bolster my physical and psychological growth. I developed a routine of working out six hours every day, lifting weights and playing racquetball but mostly working out at the karate studio. Though I held a strong resolve to remain uninfluenced by any consciousness-altering substances, I felt inexplicably drawn to reading all of the Carlos Castaneda books for a second time, and they mesmerized me even stronger than before. Not only did I read them all again but I was so enthralled that I also read everything written about them, including works critical of them.

When I finished the Castaneda books, I devoured other spiritual books until I felt as if I couldn't read any more, because they all seemed to be saying the same thing. I thought it might be time for me to say something of my own. After taking a creative writing course as part of my college work, I discovered that I had a passion for the written word. I had written songs and poetry and now enjoyed writing to the point of crafting longer nonfiction pieces that I submitted to inspirational magazines. I started getting published on a regular basis.

After a year at the karate studio, I met a guy who started training as a white belt. Recently divorced, Steve had just moved to Southern California from Boston and knew all about Dorchester. He also played music and rode a motorcycle. We became instant friends and took our motorcycles on long trips into the mountains. Steve lived close to the karate studio and gave me the keys to his apartment so I could shower after workouts, and he told me I could come and go whenever I wanted. We spent a lot of time together until he found a girlfriend. After he told me about her, I didn't hear from him as much, which I expected, so I backed off to give him time with his new love and occupied myself with my own pursuits. When I didn't hear from him for a few weeks, I checked in and got no answer at his apartment, so I called him at work.

A woman answered, and when I asked for him, she acted strangely, saying, "Who are you and what do you want?"

Mystified over her odd behavior, I said, "I'm a good friend of Steve's from karate. Can I talk to him?"

She hesitated for a long awkward moment before saying, "Steve just got killed on his motorcycle."

"How?"

"He pulled out into traffic, lost traction on some gravel, and slid over to the other side of the street, where an oncoming car hit and killed him. His father has flown out from Boston to recover his body. He's put together a gathering in his honor tonight at a hotel."

Steve's sudden, unexpected passing shocked me. Dazed, I rode my motorcycle to the gathering in a gesture to honor him in my own way. When I arrived I walked into a large crowd of people from his work and other parts of his life, realizing that I didn't know a soul. I didn't know what to say or do, so I watched for a few minutes, figuring out who his father was. I started to approach him two or three times but felt separate and isolated, so I turned around and left, taking a long motorcycle ride home, puzzling over Steve's death. Since I came from Dorchester, many of my friends had died, some murdered and some in tragic accidents, but it had been years since death had confronted me. Fresh from his divorce, Steve had been creating a new life full of promise, and in one brief flash, death wiped it all out.

I slid into a dark funk that I could not escape. Days, weeks, and months passed while I waited for the inevitable bounce that would bring me back from my depression, but it didn't come. Steve's death haunted me day and night, shrouding every moment of my life with an oppressive weight that I could not get out from under. As time passed, an idea slowly formed: a way to honor and immortalize Steve while dealing with the burden of his passing. I had no idea what I was doing, but the idea of a book germinated in my mind, so I wrote, knowing it would be cathartic.

Using legal pads and pencils, I meticulously printed each word, filling pad after pad with a story about a man who gets killed on his motorcycle and wakes up outside his body. Remembering the possessed look in my friend Wayne's eye when he drank himself into oblivion, I explored the theme. In the afterlife my character meets other disincarnate spirits who teach him how to slip into the bodies of the living, temporarily possessing them in moments of lowered consciousness when they drank too much. Using these bodies, they experienced physical pleasures again and caused all kinds of havoc before leaving the bodies behind without having to suffer the consequences of their actions. The possessed person awoke with hangover and no memory of anything they had done. My protagonist didn't know that his supposed mentors were demons, teaching him to possess unsuspecting victims.

I spent five years writing and rewriting my book twice by hand, getting carpal tunnel syndrome for my efforts. Music took a back seat to my obsession, but I continued in karate, growing in confidence until I felt like I didn't have to carry a knife anymore.

I went through a couple of jobs until I found one repairing computers that required extensive travel. I liked it because I worked from home, rarely seeing my boss, and when business slowed, I could stay home and write. While on the road, the solitude of travel and hotels gave me ample uninterrupted time to write. After landing this job, I sold some stock from my first company and purchased my first house. As if to catalyze these big changes in my life, the karate studio closed down soon afterward.

After five years writing two drafts in longhand, I had taken my book as far as I could. While out walking late one night, after having dinner in another part of town, I saw a writer's bookstore advertising read-and-critique workshops. I signed up for an all-day Saturday session and read my first chapter to a half a dozen older women who tore what I had written to shreds. Afterward the workshop leader kindly offered to take my first three chapters home with him to give them a closer, more personal criticism.

A few weeks later, I received my chapters back, and to my dismay the workshop leader said the same things the women had, only he said them nicer. Disgusted, I tossed the chapters into the corner on top of the pile of two drafts of handwritten legal pads, justifying it to myself by thinking that none of them recognized my talent. My five years of hard work meant nothing and the writing business proved to be a waste of time.

I was through.

THIRTY-ONE

Getting It Write

I walked past the pile in the corner several times in the weeks that followed. Once my rage subsided, I felt a pull from my work that grew with each passing day. Finally I picked up the chapters and criticisms and looked them over again, thinking maybe there's truth in some of what they said. Based on their criticisms, I rewrote my first chapter and went back to the bookstore to read it to a writing workshop that met once a week. They butchered it again, but not as bad as my first outing. I went home and rewrote it based on their suggestions and returned the following week for more criticism and another rewrite. After six readings and rewrites, they told me not to bring it back anymore.

I came back the following week with my second chapter and from that point on I came to the workshop once a week, each time reading a new chapter. In this ongoing workshop, I discovered a group of writers dedicated to helping each other, and we gelled into a special family who gave tough, honest criticism.

My critical skills and the depth of my literary analysis grew quickly while the quality of my writing improved. A few months after settling into the group, I attended my first writer's conference; a small one where I came close to winning a fiction award. Heartened by the positive response to my work, I registered for one of the biggest and oldest writer's conferences in the country that went for a week. Its writing workshops ran almost twenty-four hours a day.

True to form, I tried to do all of the workshops and reached burnout and exhaustion halfway through the week, along with a bitter disappointment from a literary agent who expressed enthusiasm for my work, only to reject me, literally overnight. Though defeated, I came out of the conference with a new mentor who took me under her wing after reading samples of my work. I joined her weekly workshop and attended two different writing workshops a week. My new mentor taught me writing and editing techniques that brought me to a higher level.

In my quest to write "tighter," I took a short story writing course along with my two workshops so I could learn how to say more using fewer words. I started writing short stories that explored horror and dark science fiction themes, a far cry from the inspirational nonfiction I had previously published. As part of my fascination with the dark aspects of human nature, I felt drawn to researching vampires and werewolves, which led me to lycanthropy, the basis for the werewolf mythos. At its heart is the ancient belief of numerous world cultures in the ability of humans to transform into animals, more commonly known as shape shifting. My research into shape shifting led me to its roots in shamanism, and nowhere did this become more apparent than in South America. At the core of South American shamanism, I discovered the ancient, widespread use of visionary plants. My joyful discovery resonated with the writings of Carlos Castaneda.

My writing took on a new direction that drew me inexorably toward a consuming fascination with botany. I had been a vegetarian for more than a dozen years, but I had not taken anything that altered me physiologically or psychologically in more than a decade. My research gave me the idea for a novel about a man who discovered that he could change his physical form into any animal he chose. I wanted the story to have some grain of truth to anchor it in the real world so readers could more easily accept the reality I wanted to create. The use of visionary plants among the people of South America gave me the basis for my premise and drove the focus of my research. Motivated by my desire for authenticity, I submerged myself in the University of California library system, absorbing everything I could about visionary plants.

Three of them caught my attention. First San Pedro, one of the most ancient of the magic plants of South America known as Huachuma. This mescaline-containing cactus is still used in modern times by medicine men in the coastal regions and the Andes of Peru and Bolivia.

The second plant, Datura, is a deadly narcotic plant with a long history as a medicine and sacred hallucinogen found in Mexico, the American Southwest, China, Africa, and many other places.

The third, most striking plant indigenous to the Amazon is a plant called ayahuasca, known as the vine of death, the vine of the soul, caapi, yajé, and many other names. Ayahuasca's origins go deep into prehistory. Often found growing in the form of a DNA double helix, the ayahuasca vine is usually mixed with the leaves from a bush called chacruna or other plants containing Dimethyltryptamine, DMT for short. DMT is a powerful psychoactive substance that occurs naturally in the human brain. One of the first alkaloids isolated from the vine, initially named telepathine, intrigued me because of its reputed telepathic powers. Armed with my new knowledge of these plants, I wrote the novel I envisioned and garnered some interest from publishers and agents, but it never sold.

I fell into the habit of writing short stories between novels to keep refining my fiction writing skills. Everything I wrote had a dark aspect and a strong *Twilight Zone* influence. People classified what I wrote as horror, but my intention came from my drive to explore fear and examine the shadow side of human nature. In all of the dark fiction that I wrote, all of my monsters were human.

It had been eighteen years since I had first taken LSD and ten years since I had taken anything at all. I never forgot the terror I experienced during my first LSD experiences while peaking, the time when the acid really kicked in, making thoughts, forms, and mental imagery come faster and faster. The volume, density, speed, and sheer mass of these overwhelming abstract, multicolored, geometric thoughts and progressions drove me and most others beyond rationality and intellectual comprehension. My greatest fear came from the thought that I would indeed "lose my mind" and never return from the psychic maelstrom I had unleashed.

Armed with the memory of this terror and my newly discovered knowledge of visionary plants and shamanism, I wrote a horror story about a reckless adventurer who went to South America in search of the ultimate trip. After encountering a shaman who gave him what he asked for, the reckless adventurer indulged in the shaman's gift with complete disregard for any of the shaman's warnings about the consequences of not making a proper sacrifice. A couple of months later, he scores some unusual drugs in Central Park from a shady character and soon finds himself tripping heavily at his girlfriend's apartment. The peak of his trip keeps coming and building in intensity until he loses his mind in wild hallucinations that cause him to kill his girlfriend. The story ends with him strapped to a table, dying in a straight jacket, still peaking.

I returned to the big writer's conference where I had been devastated the year before. One of the workshop leaders took manuscripts in advance and read them out loud in her workshop so no one knew who wrote them, insuring that everyone would give and received honest, unbiased criticism. When she read my story, it garnered a standing ovation and I won a fiction award from this major writer's conference that had only given awards and workshops for literary works, mysteries, screenplays, and other mainstream works, but none quite like mine. When the workshop leader told the group that I had written it, a number of people who had taken LSD swarmed me, congratulating and encouraging me on my work.

A seventy-eight-year-old woman named Marjorie, who had a PhD in psychology, had been one of the pioneering psychiatric researchers who worked with LSD in the '50s. Marjorie had written a twenty-page report on her LSD research that had been published in a Hawaiian medical journal. She showed incredible enthusiasm for my story and begged for a copy of it, which I gave her. In return she gave me a copy of her article, an excellent piece of research, especially for the '50s.

Her bright blue eyes held a spark seldom seen in those of advanced age, and they spoke of wisdom and experience beyond that of most of her peers. She lamented to me that she couldn't relate to anyone from her generation and had few people to compare notes of her experiences with.

As a result of our meeting, Marjorie and I began corresponding. She wanted me to hear a lecture from some guy who claimed to be on the forefront of consciousness exploration and expansion. A few weeks after we exchanged letters, I received a couple of cassette tapes in the mail from her. When I finally listened to them, I heard what I can only describe as a whiny, nasal voice. I thought, *Who is this strange, possibly gay, obnoxious-sounding weirdo?* I continued listening, getting past my bias of what he sounded like, and proceeded to hear some of the most profound, expansive philosophical insights I had ever heard.

The strange, possibly gay, obnoxious-sounding weirdo turned out to be a gentleman by the name of Terence McKenna, and what Terence had to say triggered another major accelerated transformation in my life.

THIRTY-TWO

The Face of Death

Though I had been out of touch with the drug scene for more than a decade, people still came to me with questions regarding my knowledge and experiences with psychedelics. I heard about the rise of designer drugs and the horrid plague of a drug called ecstasy through the media. I felt distant from it all, yet some part of me held a fascination with altered states of consciousness that I couldn't deny. This theme kept emerging in my writing in spite of my self-imposed discipline against it, as did the concept of plants as teachers, which rang even more true in light of the fact that I had been a vegetarian for close to fifteen years. Listening to Terence McKenna stimulated my drive for spiritual development and the expansion of my consciousness: the very reason I had given everything up in the first place. In the dozen or so years since I stopped getting high, I had searched avidly—reading, studying, and meditating to further develop my spirituality—but I didn't feel like I had found the answers I wanted.

A writer friend in his mid-fifties told me he had experimented with LSD and had some unsettling experiences. He suspected that his son, a young man in his early twenties, had been experimenting with it too. He asked me if I would consider "coming out of retirement" to guide him on a journey. A week or two later, his son came to me independently, telling me of his own unsettling LSD experiences. He also asked if I would guide him on a journey and shared his suspicion that his father might be experimenting. I asked them on separate occasions if they ever considered discussing it and doing it together, and both of them said, "No way." The timing of their queries and the fact that they had come to *me* independent of each other set my mind in motion.

I rationalized that I hadn't done anything in years and I now had a more mature and objective perspective to judge my experience by. After giving the whole situation a great deal of thought, I decided that a big part of me felt duty bound to go back into the territory I knew so well to guide both father and son on a joint psychedelic experience. I spoke with both of them, arranging the set and setting for the journey, which was an uninterrupted day at the father's house. Father and son each did one and a half hits of blotter acid and I did four, figuring that if I planned to give up my years of unaltered consciousness and fly, I wanted my experience to be a strong one.

I had an incredibly wonderful, manic trip and the most fun I'd had in years. It felt like I obliterated a dam of repression that had held me for over a decade. I felt so cleansed, energized, and empowered that I planned to set a new precedent, revisiting the experience once every few years to give myself a fresh perspective.

The Gulf War broke out soon after that and they sent my neighbor, a marine who lived across the street, to the front. I kept an eye on his sixty-seven-year-old mom, Dee, in his absence and checked in with her most days, lending a hand when she needed it. With only her old dog for a companion, I could tell Dee was lonely, so I talked with her frequently.

One day she complained of chest pains after weed-whacking her yard. From the way she described it, I thought it might be muscle strain, so I mildly chastised her for not calling for help. She told me she hated asking and treasured her independence. I told her to lie down, rest, and not exert herself anymore. She agreed and followed my advice. The next morning her best friend knocked on my door, worried because she called Dee every morning and on this morning she didn't get an answer. We went to knock together and got no answer, except the frantic barking of her dog, so I decided to go in. All of the doors and windows had been locked, but I saw a shower window open on the second floor. Another neighbor brought an extension ladder, which helped me squeeze through the small window. Once inside, I heard the steady beep of an answering machine and the barking of her dog. I knew what I would find, but I had no idea how it would look.

I started down the stairs, calling her name, getting no answer but the frenzied barks of her dog, who charged at me, biting me on the hand. It wasn't a vicious skin-breaking bite but a nervous bite. The dog ran back to the end of the hall to a room on the left before turning around and charging me again. Feeling like a character in some surreal horror movie, I continued down the hall—answering machine beeping, agitated dog barking—calling out Dee's name, getting no answer from the room at the end of the hall.

The dog's frenzy increased as I approached.

I made it to the room, turned the corner, and found Dee's lifeless body scrunched up on the floor in a semi-fetal position. The smell of the room hit me with a palpable force that rocked me to my core: dog, death, and loneliness.

Knowing I would feel nothing, I knelt down and felt her cold, stiff wrist for a nonexistent pulse. Then I went to the phone in a daze and called the cops before going to the crowd of neighbors gathered outside the front door to deliver the news. Some of them wanted to come in and check on her, but I kept them out, telling them that they didn't want to see her this way and that the cops didn't want anyone in the house.

When he came the cop gave me a hard time about breaking into the house until I explained my relationship with Dee. The coroner came a short while later and asked me to help sort through things, notify the next of kin, and seal off the house. I spent a few hours helping him and received a crash course in the legal aspects of death. Dee's death kept me numbed and in a fog. Like an endlessly looping videotape, the impact of the smell that defined loneliness haunted me, as did the image of her lying on the floor while the dog barked and the answering machine incessantly beeped.

This confrontation with death fueled my sense of mortality and gave me the feeling that my life was slipping by unfulfilled. In my thirteen years of staying clean and fifteen years of being a vegetarian, I still hadn't found the answers I was looking for.

THIRTY-THREE

Plants as Teachers

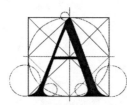 friend of the family kept bugging me to smoke cannabis with him. I thought hard about it because I didn't have many ways to deal with stress after the karate studio closed, and regular workouts didn't help. Facing death head on again had a profoundly unsettling effect on me. After an extended time feeling listless and unfulfilled, I gave in and smoked a joint.

Not only did I love it, but it made me lighten up, so I decided to smoke it occasionally; otherwise I feared the stress and depression would take their toll. I soon discovered that the politics of cannabis had changed considerably in my thirteen-year absence. When I had stopped smoking it, everyone loved the imports; among them Columbian, Panamanian, Oaxacan, commercial Mexican, and the exotic Thai stick and Hawaiian buds with names like Maui Wowee. Now with the passage of time, the domestic crop ruled, especially the buds from Humboldt

County and numerous other genetically bred superior strains of Indica and Sativa grown in indoor nurseries. Everyone grew sensimilla, the buds from potent female plants that produced maximum resin by withholding pollination. Propagated by their cuttings, these cloned plants and the high-quality smoke they produce only required one or two hits for a strong buzz.

After getting laid off from my job repairing computers, I landed a job as a research-and-development technician with a biotech company that specialized in electronic instruments. One of the guys I worked with turned out to be an indoor cannabis grower who had a three-bedroom house and a two-car garage filled with plants that he cultivated on a regular basis. He gifted me often and I had all the pot I wanted for nothing. He also taught me everything I needed to know about growing and supplied me with a couple of rooted cuttings so I could grow enough to keep myself and my friends supplied. I didn't grow anywhere near the volume that he produced and I never sold any, but I had plenty to smoke and gave out lots of gifts.

My unexpected confrontation with death shifted my thinking away from my old, rigid, self-imposed paradigm to a more open-minded perspective. I didn't have any desire to drink or get loaded in any way that deadened my awareness. I wanted to open myself and heighten my awareness, and the plants seemed to hold the answers.

Marjorie, who had been a pioneer in mind expansion, had given me a great gift by sending me Terence McKenna's lectures. What I learned from them had planted a seed in my mind regarding the religious use of plants, and these insights led me to read his brilliant book, *The Food of the Gods*. In it, Terence put forth factual proof of plants used as sacraments that provided the basis and vehicle for visionary experience. All of my personal research during thirteen years of staying clean brought me to this fundamental truth.

Visionaries, mystics, and prophets provided the core for all of the world's religions. Their roots originated with shamans, the original prehistoric masters of inducing and navigating altered states of consciousness that went back to the beginnings of humanity and its awe with the divine source of all creation.

How else could anyone achieve ecstatic states aside from fasting, self-flagellation, sleep deprivation, or self-mutilation, and why go through all that when the simple ingestion of a plant created by God could bring the same results? Jesus Christ went into the desert and fasted for forty days and forty nights to see God, because Jesus himself played the role of a shaman. If anyone was inclined to fast for forty days and forty nights in the desert, I have no doubt that they would see God too. A bold concept took root in my mind in the form of a question, and the more I considered it, the more it drew me in because it made sense in spite of the fact that everything I had encountered and learned in Western society went against it.

Did I dare think that a consciousness-altering psychedelic experience could provide the basis for a religious experience?

Pondering it, I could only come up with yes as my answer, simply because it made sense. I came to this conclusion after thirteen years of spiritual searching as a vegetarian who would not even drink soda or coffee or take aspirin.

Plants grew on the earth before animals, which could not exist without plants. If the animals disappeared, the plants would continue living, but if the plants disappeared, man and the animals would die off from starvation and lack of oxygen. The expression "dumb as a house plant" has become a cliché, but which form of life *really* holds the greater wisdom? If by chance plants were the keepers of ancient knowledge, then how would they communicate?

Through external means they speak to us with shapes, colors, and scents, but when we ingest certain teachers among them, they speak through colors, patterns, abstractions, and archetypes, introducing concepts beyond limited rational thinking. Moreover, the language of teacher plants unfolds their cosmic wisdom, blossoming in geometric permutations that speak in mathematical progressions using the universal language of sacred geometry to reveal the true nature of the divine unfolding of conscious intelligence that permeates all that is.

After years of being out of touch with psychedelic substances and the horror stories I heard about drugs from the media, I knew the general public wouldn't understand the conclusion I came to. From all of the extensive research I had done, I knew that shamans had mastered the art of navigating these altered states of consciousness.

Mircea Eliade, one of the foremost anthropologists of the twentieth century, titled his seminal book: *Shamanism – Archaic Techniques of*

Ecstasy. What I learned from my research is that shamans were the first teachers, healers, musicians, performing artists, storytellers, doctors, and mystics who provided the core of the world's religious thought. I could find no rational arguments to dispute what intuitively made sense to me. The only opposition against deeper inner explorations on my part came from the legal issues that our fear-based society enforced, but my yearning for the answers to my life's meaning overrode any fear I had of legal ramifications.

I had to know for myself.

I believed that the plants held the answers, but I had no way of knowing how to get them until I saw a book in a head shop one day entitled *Psilocybin: Magic Mushroom Grower's Guide: A Handbook for Psilocybin Enthusiasts* by O. T. Oss and O. N. Oeric. I didn't know it at the time, but Oss and Oeric turned out to be Terence McKenna and his brother Dennis.

I bought the book and soon found myself drawing up plans for growing mushrooms, thinking of it like a science fair project. I knew that if I followed through with the plan forming in my mind, I had to keep my deeper inquiries and activities to myself. I felt no one would understand my obsession with growing mushrooms and ingesting them the way the ancients did, as a sacrament.

From Terence I learned that the Aztecs called them *teonanácatl,* which meant "flesh of the gods."

THIRTY-FOUR

Flesh of the Gods

I spent more than a thousand dollars buying a pressure cooker, lab ware, agar, and other materials necessary to grow hallucinogenic mushrooms from spores. After hours of hard exacting work and two failed attempts, I harvested my first flush of three ounces of dried Psilocybe cubensis mushrooms. I waited for a weekend night that felt good and ate five grams of mushrooms, scarcely believing that I had grown them and skeptical that they would have any effect. When first exposed to them, I had been an inexperienced teenager pushing the boundaries in a haphazard, thrill-seeking way. Now, at the age of forty, I approached "the flesh of the gods" with respect and a serious spiritual intention, backed by years of in-depth research into shamanism.

I had a wonderful, joy-filled, gentle journey of rediscovery, heralded by the mushrooms coming on in rising waves that made me giddy. I saw soft, beautiful colors, unfolding geometric patterns, and wonderful blue, pink, and gold neon filigrees around much of what I looked at. I felt very conscious of looking at the world through a different set of perceptions. I flashed on my early psychedelic experiences, when I had forbidden myself from having sexual thoughts because of my fear that I would damage my chromosomes. Now I understood that this irrational fear had been put into me by the lies and misinformation of our government.

Now the lies had no power.

This time out I wanted to experience as many things as possible while under the spell of the mushrooms. My stainless steel drum set, bathed in colorful highlights, called to me and I remembered how much I liked to play under the influence of LSD, so I went with the urge and sat down to play to my heart's delight, inspired by the mushrooms. Playing my drums gave me a whole new perspective on music, drumming, and my relationship to all of it. After I played, my mind spun off in a flurry of multiple directions. I wanted to go outside and experience nature; I wanted to walk someplace; I wanted to hear different music, see other things through new eyes…

I stumbled around the house, trying to change my clothes, my desires shifting with each moment, carrying my body in one direction until a new thought came along, changing it once again. I tried to do too many things too fast, to the point of tripping myself up in the hallway with my pants down around my ankles, which sent me tumbling to the floor in laughter. Anyone watching would have thought me out of my mind, but in truth my mind moved too fast for my body. I made myself lie on the floor until I put some order to my wishes. Then I followed through with what I wanted to see, feel, hear, touch, and smell until the effect of the mushrooms diminished, leaving me satisfied and looking forward to more experiences.

I took mushrooms frequently after that, upping the dose from the original five to seven grams, sometimes taking as many as nine, all the while pushing the envelope harder and higher. Higher doses brought more intense journeys that often passed through fear-based periods of darkness when the first powerful waves washed over me. I felt this lurking darkness as an unsettling alien presence. Higher doses also made me aware of hidden things in the darkness that needed attention because they made me feel fear by magnifying it, which meant I had to pursue it. I worked through the dark energies every chance I could, but I didn't realize their awesome power until much later.

After many solo journeys, I felt compelled to share the incredible insights I received, so I began talking about them with a few close friends. Like my writer friend and his son, more of my friends asked me to guide them on journeys. Looking back, I should have given them three or four grams of mushrooms for starters instead of seven, but I didn't realize what a "hard head" I had become. I always took more mushrooms than the person I guided so they would realize that no matter what happened, I had taken more than they had and I could still function and guide them. I felt that this practice acted as a psychological buffer for people new to the experience. All of them benefited from my higher-dose approach, but I scared a few.

Over time I realized that it's more beneficial to start people lower and build them up to higher doses if they desire. Mushrooms at low doses increase visual acuity and edge perception. At higher doses they bring full-on visionary experience. Anyone serious about working with them should experience the whole range of doses, building from low to high, as each have their own unique qualities.

During this time of burgeoning self-discovery, I grew my own cannabis and mushrooms, which I kept to myself and a few close friends. Keeping it under wraps allowed me to have my own supply of sacraments without interacting with other people and attracting the wrong attention. That kept me safe, isolated, and out of touch with anything happening on a larger scale until I walked into a head shop one day and saw a copy of *High Times* magazine.

That thing's still around? I thought incredulously.

Something made me flip it open right to a page with an ad for a weekend conference on shamanic plant sciences to be held in San Francisco. My barely contained excitement spilled over when I recognized the names of the speakers presenting at the seminar: the very same people whose work I had read on my own during my forays into the University of California libraries researching shamanism and visionary plants. I didn't have much money, but it didn't matter. This moment had way too much synchronicity to ignore. Seeing *High Times* after twenty years constituted a minor revelation, but flipping it open directly to an ad and recognizing most of the names from my own independent research brought all of my life's work to a nexus point. No matter the price, I *had* to be there.

I charged my plane fare, hotel, transportation, and the fee for the seminar all on my credit card, and soon after I arrived, I charged another 550 dollars to *Mind Books* book store, filling two shopping bags with books on shamanism and entheobotany. More importantly, I walked into a huge auditorium and saw well over a thousand like-minded souls.

I didn't realize it at the time, but I had discovered the tribe.

THIRTY-FIVE

The Four Ds

thnobotany is the study of humanity's relationship to plants. Entheobotany is a more specific discipline that studies humanity's sacred and religious relationship to plants, which in the distant past came under the domain of the shamans. This specific focus branches out into a fascinating amalgam of other disciplines that includes chemists, botanists, neurologists, doctors, psychiatrists, anthropologists, archeologists, philosophers, artists, writers, and musicians. In short, it merges spiritual, creative, and scientific expertise.

Theo is the Latin root of the word that means "God," and *entheo* means "the God within;" along with the word *botany*, which applies to the plants. So the essence and meaning of Entheobotany is "the God within the plant that brings out the God within you."

LSD, mushroom, and mescaline usage by Timothy Leary, Aldous Huxley, Ken Kesey, Alan Ginsberg, and the rest of the ground-breaking consciousness researchers of the last half of the twentieth century helped solidify the word *psychedelic* to describe visionary mind-altering substances. This word originated because the initial rediscovery of these plant sacraments made researchers believe they could use psychedelics to mimic psychosis and allow a closer study of it. Unfortunately the word's origins and Kesey and Leary's highly publicized run-ins with the law, along with all of the negative connotations—including drugs, bad trips, hippies, and the supposed breakdown and moral decay of society—caused a knee-jerk reaction from authorities that led to the paranoid and senseless war on drugs.

Visionary experience and plant sacraments formed the basis for Christianity and then became repressed by organized Christianity for hundreds of years in the form of inquisitions, witch hunts, and the persecution of shamans. With the reintroduction of mind-expanding substances into a spiritually starved society, people no longer accepted the spoon-fed lies of the government. Instead they questioned war, authority, consumer culture, and the conformity of accepted social norms.

At the end of the twentieth century, the entheobotanists coined a new name for plant sacraments, naming them *entheogens* to give them the respect they deserved. These highly educated individuals from many fields of study came together to make entheobotany the core of the formation of the tribe, and Terence McKenna became the Pied Piper, touching the souls of those who heard his message. Terence coined the term "the Archaic Revival," and it had begun.

Most people who considered themselves part of the tribe gave Terence credit for getting their attention. Now I found myself among them at an entheobotany seminar, feeling instant recognition of like-minded people and an unusual sense of connection, much like I had with the writing community, only different in ways I couldn't articulate. My only problem came from not knowing anybody. I knew from experience that I might have difficulty getting "in" due to the controversial legal status of mind-altering substances. I couldn't just walk up to someone and say, "Hi. You know where I can score some LSD?"

I attended the seminar for long days packed full of lectures, taking copious notes, sucking up all the knowledge I could from each presenter. In between breaks I wandered the booths and vendor tables until late in the seminar, when I overheard a couple of guys talking

psychedelic magazine they wanted to publish in Southern
nia. When the discussion ended, I introduced myself, telling
had overheard their conversation and that I was a writer myself.
Mark, the editor of the magazine, introduced himself to me. Then he
introduced Ron, the publisher, and we traded phone numbers. Aside
from being the magazine's editor, Mark studied comparative religion
and had extensive knowledge of the use of visionary plants throughout
the history of the world's religions. Soon after returning from the
seminar, he invited me to a weekly potluck at a big house he shared
with half a dozen other students. A good crowd came and the potluck
ended in a fun, energetic drum circle.

In parallel with my new discoveries, I worked long hours at a new
job, repairing computers for a big corporation. I did mushrooms on
weekends, integrating my experiences with what I read about the plants.
On Tuesdays I attended Mark's potlucks and furthered my research on
shamanism in intellectual and experiential ways, while writing a historical
novel about shamanism. My day job took a tremendous amount of
energy. The managers I worked for were incompetent and the whole
computer repair center had gone to a shambles. My upper manager left
and they removed my immediate boss from his job. I ended up working
for a coworker who proved to be more incompetent than our former
boss, which added to my frustration, but the upper manager's position
went to my close friend Rob, who had helped me get my job.

I knew I could straighten things out and make the computer lab
work more efficiently, but I felt awkward because of my friendship with
Rob. I didn't want to be accused of, or be guilty of, nepotism, but when
my long hours and frustrations intruded on my sleep, I found myself
awake at two thirty one morning with a full-blown plan mapping itself
out in my mind. I sat down and started writing, filling six single-spaced
pages, venting my frustrations and stating what I would do to fix the
problems if I had the authority and resources. Then I emailed it to Rob
and went in to work.

By the end of that day, he did everything I suggested. Then he
put me in charge of the computer repair lab, making me responsible
for more than five thousand computer users in eighteen different
locations. At that point the lab had miserable satisfaction ratings and
had fallen two hundred thousand dollars in the hole. I worked even

harder, putting in longer hours until I injured my lower back from overwork and stress, which laid me out flat for more than a month. People who worked for me came to visit and I communicated using email more than I should have because I didn't want to let Rob down. As a result of my efforts and the people I hired, in less than a year's time I had improved the lab's financials from a two-hundred-thousand-dollar deficit to a thirty-thousand-dollar positive variance, and we had pulled the lab's satisfaction ratings up to 98 percent.

During this transition it occurred to me that I lived in three radically different worlds that I could move in and out of with ease. I supervised a computer lab for a corporate high-tech government contractor, I wrote fiction, and I became a well-known writing teacher and member of the writing community. I had also become part of the psychedelic tribe, respected as a serious and experienced psychonaut, a term consciousness researchers use to define an inner traveler motivated by the same spirit of exploration into the unknown that makes astronauts travel outward.

I worked long days and saw Mark once a week, attending potlucks and listening to university-sponsored lecturers who came to speak on comparative religion and plant sacraments. I also became the fiction editor of the psychedelic magazine, and I supplied the publisher with rebuilt computers resurrected from leftover parts from the computer lab. Mark put tremendous effort into making the magazine a reality, but Ron, the publisher, had too many personal problems that prevented it from happening in spite of Mark's hard work.

At one of Mark's gatherings, I had the honor of meeting Dr. Stanley Krippner, an eminent psychologist who had strong connections to the Grateful Dead and Rolling Thunder, the shaman. Stan had spent time with shamans from every culture imaginable and provided a fount of knowledge while being very supportive of my work. His analysis of shamanic reality made the most sense to me. He said that if you break shamanism down to its core, it consisted of four basic elements that he called the four Ds of shamanism:

Dancing.
Drumming.
Drugs.
Dreaming.
The more I pondered them, the more sense they made.

THIRTY-SIX

True History and the Roots of the Archaic Revival

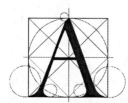ncient religions and civilizations always held a strong fascination for me, but the watered-down Christianity-dictated public-school version of "history" I had been taught only revealed shadows of the truth. History as we know it began with the written word, recorded primarily by the male-dominated conquering cultures. Unfortunately the conquered rarely get to reveal their origins because the conquering cultures have attacked the core of their belief systems in hopes of destroying every trace of history and culture they could find.

In light of the historical truths that I rediscovered, especially those concerned with the use of plant sacraments, my concepts of time and history took on a whole new perspective—based on the roots of shamanism. Pagan goddess religions, the sacredness of life, the unity of all things and the vast, intricate relationship of humanity, and all life on earth to the greater unseen forces of the cosmos all started coming into focus. The time had come for the cosmic feminine to reassert herself.

Astronomers, astrologers, mathematicians, alchemists, herbalists, and midwives whom the Christians burned, tortured, and persecuted as witches were the priests and priestesses of Mother Earth. Things that I had been taught to look upon with derision took on new significance. These allegedly superstitious shadow beliefs of humanity made up the ancient, culturally sublimated elements that became the major expressions of the Archaic Revival.

In the greatest of cosmic ironies, the actions that the United States government took to remain in control of everything fostered the Archaic Revival into existence while undermining the foundation the government had so painstakingly struggled to perpetuate. When the world teetered on the brink of destruction with the outbreak of World War II, the ultimate weapon of destruction became possible by harnessing the atom and manifesting its destructive power into a mushroom-cloud explosion. The fact that this weapon of destruction came in the form of a mushroom-shaped cloud carried great significance. Mushrooms are a fungus that grows at the point of decomposition at the junction of life and death, transforming spent life back into basic organic substances.

While Hitler terrorized Europe, Albert Hofmann, an organic chemist working for Sandoz Laboratories in neutral Switzerland worked with another fungus called Claviceps purpurea that grows on rye plants in an effort to isolate its vasoconstrictor properties to help women who hemorrhaged in childbirth. While most of the world focused on death, Albert Hofmann focused on life.

In 1938 he produced LSD 25, the twenty-fifth permutation of Lysergic Acid Diethylamide, and deemed it to have no research value. After he put it on the shelf for five years, an intuition prompted him to take another look at it. Somewhere in the process of handling it, Albert had an experience on Friday, April 16, 1943 that made him feel odd and different. Being a good scientist, he suspected that his odd feelings might be related to the LSD he had synthesized, so on Monday, April 19, 1943, at 4:20 p.m., Albert Hofmann ingested 250 micrograms of LSD, which he thought of as a miniscule dose. This amount turned out to be a mind-blowing dose that changed him and the world as we know it forever.

Albert Hofmann and Sandoz Laboratories made LSD freely available to scientists in the psychiatric community as a possible aid to psychotherapy and for possible treatment of schizophrenia and other forms of psychosis. The Central Intelligence Agency in the United States showed particular interest in it, but the CIA had no interest in the possible healing properties of this powerful mind-altering substance. They wanted to explore the possibilities of using it as an agent for psychological warfare and mind control.

A few short years later, an international banker by the name of Gordon Wasson, who had dedicated his life to the study of mushrooms, came in contact with an ancient mushroom cult in Oaxaca, Mexico that had been suppressed by Christian zealots for four hundred years. Wasson became the first Westerner to ingest the mushrooms with a *curandera* by the name of Maria Sabina, a keeper of the mushroom secret. Wasson reported his findings in a now famous Life Magazine article dated June 10, 1957 that dubbed the Psilocybe cubensis mushrooms "the magic mushrooms of Mexico." Wasson sent samples of the mushrooms to Albert Hofmann, who isolated the active component, naming it Psilocybin. Unbeknownst to Wasson, the CIA had partially funded his expedition through a front organization and sent an undercover operative with him. Like with their interest in LSD, the CIA wanted to explore the possibilities of using Psilocybin as an agent for psychological warfare.

Albert Hofmann's process of creating LSD centered around extracting it from the Claviceps purpurea fungus. The CIA wanted Sandoz to synthesize it for them, but to their credit, Sandoz declined, so the CIA paid Parke Davis, an American pharmaceutical company, to do the work, and Parke Davis delivered. In their misguided quest, the CIA initiated project MK Ultra, which ultimately led to experiments on themselves, the military, and the public in general. Covertly, with taxpayer dollars, the CIA ran a string of whore houses with one-way mirrors where the johns were secretly dosed with LSD by the prostitutes and observed through one-way mirrors.

Through the clandestine efforts of the United States government, LSD filtered into the general public. On the West Coast, Ken Kesey took LSD in a research study that inspired him to start a group called the Merry Pranksters, who traveled cross country in a bus named "Furthur," dosing everyone they could find with LSD in what came to be known as the Electric Kool-Aid Acid Test.

On the East Coast, Timothy Leary, a Harvard psychologist who first discovered the mushroom experience poolside in Mexico, embarked on the infamous Harvard Psilocybin project, which soon turned to LSD. Unable to keep the experience within the confines of Harvard's rules, Leary and his project were banished. This sent him on his own mission to spread the psychedelic holy grail with the famous admonition, "Turn on, tune in, and drop out."

The United States government's secretive efforts at psychological warfare to further the testosterone-fueled, aggressive model of war, destruction, and domination, blew up in their face like the mushroom cloud of the atomic bomb, fueling the anti-war movement with peace, love, and flower power.

I found myself blessed to be swept up in the tail end of this movement in 1971, after LSD became illegal, when we could buy powerful four-way hits manufactured at the Massachusetts Institute of Technology, known as MIT, or as we used to say, Mental Institute for the Touched. Thanks to the efforts of the US government, I tripped my brains out every other night for months on end from 1971 until I went into the military in early 1974. After a year and a half in the belly of the beast, I came in contact with LSD again, but it had gone down considerably in potency. Now, through my friends Ron, Mark, and others in the tribe, I found sources of LSD, which I took with a more conscious intention, furthering my explorations into my inner life, the world, and the expanding universe that I found myself at the center of.

Many people came to me after seeing the changes I experienced and asked me to lead them on their first experiences. After careful screening and laying down strict rules regarding "set" and "setting," I introduced them to new ways of perceiving and being in the world. All of them felt transformed and thankful for the guidance and the experience.

I still rejected Christianity and considered myself more of a pagan than anything else. I abhorred anything having to do with organized religion and saw their rituals as a far cry from what I thought of as spirituality. One Saturday night on the eve of an Easter Sunday, I took a large dose of LSD and stayed up all night, having a wonderful mystical and cathartic experience around the real meaning of Easter. I had been invited to a massive sunrise service at a major California theme park, and on a last-minute inspiration, while still very much under the influence of the LSD, I joined my brother and his family for the service. At the Christian ceremony, I saw the trappings of its pagan roots interwoven through its rituals and felt an ancient connection in the voices raised up in song, praising the creator. The beauty of those voices brought me to tears as I grasped the full meaning of Easter.

The death and rebirth of Jesus, blooming lilies, Easter eggs, Easter bunnies, and baby chicks all represented the pagan fertility rites of spring, reproduction, and renewal within the continuous cosmic cycles of life and death that surround us. Easter signifies a miracle of life and rebirth worthy of celebration no matter what religious orientation one might have. The truth of it became crystal clear to me amid the joyful tears that welled up from deep within, cementing my understanding of the oneness and connectedness of all that is.

THIRTY-SEVEN

Synchronicities

he more I used psychedelics with conscious intent, the more magical my life became, but it was a slow and gradual unfolding, and not without pain. My first magical experiences both thrilled and unnerved me when they instantaneously made the world around me feel dreamlike and unreal. They came sporadically through the years, often connected with something I was reading, as if guiding me by spirit to an insight that I sought or needed. Many months later, I sat at home looking at a small table I had, thinking how I would arrange some seemingly innocuous objects that I had collected on it. I had a quartz crystal, feathers, and a few other stones I had gathered without knowing why, along with some smaller items people had given me. I became engrossed, taking great care to arrange things just so. The thought of my display being an altar struck me the moment I finished, then I went to the couch to stretch out with a book about shamanism.

Plopping myself down, I picked up the book and flipped open to my bookmarked page.

I felt my entire world drop out from beneath me when I saw the first words on the page describing what makes up a shaman's altar. I read on incredulously as the very items I had just taken so much care to arrange were described, while wave after wave of stunned disbelief hammered me. I became disoriented and found myself standing, sitting, and standing again, then pacing in circles, trying to comprehend what had happened. How would anyone believe it, and whom could I tell without them thinking me delusional?

The impact of what I alone knew in my heart to be a sign from spirit first frightened, then excited me with the rush of implications and realizations that flooded in behind it. It took a long time for me to settle down while my seeming afterthought of an altar became a reality whose power I now respected and looked at with new wonder. This incident gave me one of those rare moments in life when I had spent a long time knocking on Spirit's door, and when I least expected it, spirit answered by knocking back and scaring the shit out of me. After this synchronistic "initiation," spirit came knocking with greater frequency when I least expected it in a manner that touched me in profound and transformative ways.

Having discovered the tribe at the entheobotany seminar in San Francisco in nineteen ninety six, I heard about a week-long entheobotany conference to be held near some Maya ruins in Mexico. Terence McKenna and a group of the world's foremost authorities on shamanism, anthropology, botany, chemistry, and psychotherapy were scheduled to lecture. I felt an overwhelming urge to attend so I could learn more about the world's oldest religion, and I wanted to meet Terence McKenna.

I tried for a scholarship but was refused, so I planned and saved for the next conference at the beginning of 1998, scheduled to be held at the Maya ruins in Uxmal Yucatan. I had never been that far from the United States and had only spent a few hours stepping over the borders into Mexico and Canada. I didn't know anyone who would be going and I knew no Spanish, but my drive to attend outstripped my fears.

I listened to basic Spanish tapes every day on the way to and from work, updated my passport, and geared myself up for an adventure that would bring even more dramatic changes into my life. Unsure of the language and feeling particularly vulnerable because of my lack of understanding, I made my way to Uxmal after spending the night in Merida on the Yucatan peninsula. The next day I found my way to the hotel, where I roomed with a champion weightlifter, which seemed incongruous at a conference based on shamanism and altered states of consciousness. While there I had the joy and honor of meeting Terence McKenna and spending the week listening to his brilliant lectures. I gifted him with a short-story collection I had published and told him the story of the sweet little old lady who had sent me the tapes of his lectures, which ultimately brought me to Uxmal to connect with him.

I had another powerful synchronicity touring the ruins there. While walking I felt awe and respect for the spirit of the intelligence whose essences imbued the whole place with its energy. Somewhere mid-tour I had the strong thought flash through my mind, saying, *I wonder what the spirits of this place think about all these people coming here under the influence of mind-altering substances. I wonder if they think of the psychedelic pilgrimage that I am part of as being disrespectful.*

No sooner did I complete the thought when I heard the oohs and ahs of those around me while others pointed behind me, saying, "Look!" I turned around and felt like I couldn't have gotten a more definitive answer to my questions when I beheld one of the most beautiful and perfect rainbows I had ever seen. One end of it came right out of the top of the famed magician's pyramid, arcing all the way across the sky, back to the ground again.

I considered it a blessing.

While in Uxmal I learned more about substances I already knew about, numerous methods of ingestion of other substances—some new, some ancient—and still more about substances I had never experienced. I could barely keep pace with the influx of knowledge that the lecturers presented. I learned that the ancient Maya made a drink out of Psilocybin mushrooms, chocolate, honey, and morning glory seeds that contained lysergic acid, a psychoactive in its own right, and I learned about many different psychoactive mushrooms and their cultivation. I couldn't wait to get home and try my own version of the mushroom, chocolate, and morning glory cocktail.

I had my first experience smoking Salvia divinorum, a member of the sage family found in the Mexican state of Oaxaca. A hit or two of it smoked put me into an interesting, colorful, patterned visual space, but it didn't "talk" to me the way other substances did.

I also heard about 5 methoxydimethyltryptamine for the first time. 5MEO could be obtained legally and had the reputation of providing one of the most profound experiences possible. This piqued my interest, especially when my roommate, the champion weightlifter, came back to our room visibly shaken and thoroughly terrified from his experience—all from a single smoked hit of it.

I tried to get him to describe his experience, but he couldn't articulate it. Picking up on what he told me, I asked him if it was like looking God straight in the eye, and he emphatically told me yes and that he would never do it again, which only fueled my longing to try it. Someone gave me the address of where to purchase it through the mail, and I resolved to get some. I figured I had seen enough terror and darkness in my life to withstand anything.

My magical mystery tour of Uxmal ended on a literal high note when someone paid off the guards to let us into the ruins at night. A brother named Stuart from Australia gifted me with two and a half hits of LSD and a group of us went to the ruins in the darkness and had an extra special journey that swallowed me into the fabric and essence of the whole place. My peak came when I climbed to the top of the magician's pyramid and sat beside Stuart, who played the didgeridoo, adding another layer of supernatural wonder to one of the Maya centers of power. Feeling like a little boy, I spent the rest of the night frolicking through the ruins, experiencing them in many different ways until the Mexican guards grew tired of our shenanigans and began firing their guns in the air to chase us off.

During the course of that week and on that night in particular, I found a new friend and fellow explorer named Jacques who lived a couple of hours from me. A group of us ended up watching the sunrise over the ruins from the roof of the hotel before parting ways, each of us headed back by our own paths to our homes in different parts of the world. Jacques and I made a pact to get together stateside and try some new plant concoctions we had learned about. We also agreed to get some 5MEO, and when the time presented itself, we would try it together.

THIRTY-EIGHT

Dark Night of the Soul

I returned from the magic of Uxmal to my computer repair manager's job and the ongoing struggles and frustrations of my writing career. Where I had been, what I experienced, and the people I shared it with stood in stark contrast to the steel, glass, and concrete rat's maze of where I worked, not to mention the shirt-and-tie soul-deadening nine-to-five conformity that stifled me everywhere I turned. I didn't want to be there, but I intended to cultivate the ability to walk in both worlds. I had built an organization by working long, hard hours and took pride in my accomplishments. If I could make it through this adjustment, I thought I could live in corporate America without being of it, and I might have the influence to make changes from deep within the belly of the corporate beast.

Aside from the intensity that the daily grind of my job brought, many other forces converged on me, bringing me battling into each

173

day, while the personal pressures I felt kept increasing. In a short span of time, a number of my friends died from different causes. One close woman friend just a few years older than me developed a fast-spreading cancer in October that killed her by January. I never went to see her in the hospital because I heard she had been heading toward recovery. Then she died suddenly, leaving me feeling guilty.

I felt vulnerable during this time and I had a spate of rejections for a book I had hope for, which made me feel like a failure as a writer; topped by a miserable attempt at a failed romance. In an effort to lift myself, I went back to studying martial arts and ran backward into someone in a sparring session, smacking the backs of our heads, giving myself a headache that lasted for days. To compound my personal challenges, my company hired a new chief information officer who dismantled the organization I had worked so hard to improve, and he gave me a less than standard raise. As part of his reorganization, I was forced to fire a girl who worked for me, because of her alcoholism. She had been a casual friend before I became her boss, so the firing turned out to be a stressful, emotionally charged event that left me depressed.

Everything collapsed around me, making me feel beset physically, mentally, emotionally, spiritually, and monetarily, driving me into the lowest depths of despair I had ever experienced. Floundering in my hopelessness, I broke every rule of set and setting and made every mistake possible, seeking escape in an experience beyond myself for all the wrong reasons.

The night I fired the girl fell on Friday, March 21, 1998. In my despair I thought that the spring equinox felt like the right time to visit another place. Thinking of the Maya preparations I had learned about, I blended water, honey, chocolate, and nine grams of dried Psilocybe cubensis mushrooms with thirteen Hawaiian baby woodrose seeds and sat listening to some music, waiting for the concoction to take effect.

The music sounded sad and forlorn as waves of colors and patterns flooded my mind, drawing me deeper into my sorrow until I fell into an overwhelming abyss of loss, despair, and suicidal impulses that tore at my soul and shredded my heart, shooting what remained of me into a place so horrible that its black depths defied imagination. Nothing I groped for in my mind or any other place provided anything resembling stability in my weakest and most vulnerable moment until the dark night of my soul overwhelmed me and hell swallowed me whole. I tried fleeing from the terror, but my thoughts flew faster and faster, growing increasingly hopeless and horrifying with each passing moment, becoming more chaotic, surreal, crushing, and incoherent until pure madness reigned and time lost all meaning. I knew only darkness, abandonment, dread, guilt, despair, and utter loss. Then things moved quicker. Faces of dead friends filled my mind, haunting me, while crucifixion and sacrificial images ran rampant. My whole world grew darker in every aspect. Then panic took hold.

I have splintered memories of running in circles in a dark crystal pyramid, trapped outside of time. Opposing thoughts and emotions tore me apart, taunting me to kill myself, then degrading me for not having the guts to do it. I ran into and bounced off of my back sliding-glass window, wanting to escape outside into the darkness, knowing with absolute certainty that the sun would never return and the end of the world had come. Then I ran to my back room, looking for a bayonet to pierce my penis or kill myself with because an overwhelming voice, force, or whatever told me that life and death didn't matter. At one point I grew obsessed with getting a bunch of my guns loaded and going to a public place to shoot everyone in sight to bring my own demise upon myself and others. I flashed on being a samurai in a former life, taking my own life, or a Maya, dying with honor as a sacrifice at the temple of a God, but I was a coward for not having the nerve to kill myself. Life and death; one and the same.

It didn't matter.

A palpable self-loathing swallowed me, and incomprehensibly, things grew still darker. I would never see daylight again because the world had come to an end. Then I crumpled to the floor, crying so hard that my throat hurt for days after. When I couldn't bear the crushing weight of my pain and conflict any longer, darkness swallowed me until I lost consciousness. I have no idea how long I laid face down on the floor. It could have been minutes or hours; I don't know. But I opened my eyes to the terrifying aftermath of overturned furniture. My front wood and screen doors hung wide open; a blanket on the ground, half in the house, half out. My wallet and its contents littered the floor. My keys sat on the floor at the far end of the hall.

Terrified by what my neighbors may have heard or seen, I closed and locked the doors and wandered the house in a daze of disbelief and fear. I saw that I had knocked over my stereo, and blood stained my sweatshirt. Back in my bedroom, drawers from a bureau I had left open lay smashed on the floor. I looked at myself in the bathroom mirror, shocked to see my face and arms cut up, scratched, bruised, and bleeding. Both knees had been skinned and bled too.

I felt completely alone with no one to turn to—no one to burden with my hell. I could only think of my mother. Part of me felt a deep fear for her well-being. I called and woke her at five in the morning her time on the East Coast, which meant two in the morning my time on the West Coast. When I heard her voice, something triggered inside of me, causing information too dense and too limitless to flood into me, as if I had tapped a direct line into the wellspring of all cosmic knowledge. Its force sucked me into a delusion of grandeur and I started telling my mom that I had figured out the secret of life. I only needed to start writing my thoughts from the beginning of my life to the present and I would prove to everyone the secret of life, which essentially meant the oneness of reality. The breadth and depth of the knowledge I had received felt quite profound, but it came so dense and so fast I had no time to process and integrate it. All I could do was babble.

I told her that I planned to call or e-mail the man who started my company and tell him the secret of life, and write his life story so everyone would know the truth about reality. It would be a best seller, making me wealthy beyond anyone's dreams, so all those around me would be well taken care of. I had full confidence because I had figured it all out. The power of what I "downloaded" made me say that I could create heaven with my thoughts. I explained to her how thoughts produced action, which I defined as the express result of thought moving and manifesting itself on the physical plane, proving that thought created the impetus for the action. I explained how a house is built from thought. You pick up a hammer and physically nail wood together, assembling the structure, following a blueprint that itself is the expression of thought.

I babbled to her for four hours until I felt exhausted and I realized that I had scared the shit out of her and she probably thought me a lunatic for sure. I understood conceptually, at the deepest levels of my being, the things I rambled about, but because of the sheer mass of information, my articulation fell short of adequately communicating my insights. My mom told me later that during my pontifications, she feared I might kill myself.

The crushing guilt and shame I experienced in hell left me humbled, humiliated, and shattered. I had an incredibly deep sorrow, respect, and most of all, heartfelt compassion for the brotherhood of man and felt nothing but love and empathy for my fellow beings in the aftermath of my descent into madness. I never in a million years thought that I could ever be capable of, much less be consumed by the negative, self-destructive mental experiences that almost took my life. I now understood how the John Wayne Gaceys, Jeffrey Dahmers, Charlie Mansons, and the Son of Sams of the world could come into being. I had been possessed by the terrible force of that negative energy.

The more I talked to my mom, the more I realized how much I had been rambling like a madman, so I started changing what I said to try to make her think differently about the delusional-sounding insanity I had been spouting earlier. Hours had passed and I grew more rational, to the point of feeling embarrassed. I knew that she knew I had taken something. As my energy diminished, she talked me into sleeping on my grandiose plans, and in her great wisdom, she left me an out to all the craziness I had been talking. I hung up feeling beaten in every sense of the word and collapsed into an uneasy sleep.

I woke up hours later feeling fragile, shaken, confused, and vulnerable. I passed the next few days feeling spiritually and mentally numb, but my life went on full bore, engaging me with its necessities, which entailed dealing with the demands of my job and the reorganization that had run me over. After surviving my unspeakable horror, I realized that I had indeed been to hell and experienced the proverbial dark night of the soul. Nothing I could imagine in any way, shape, or form could be worse than what I had experienced, and I realized that death might have brought release from my agony, but it only would have been temporary.

I had been screwed over and victimized in the takeover at work, but I knew I was right in principle, so there was no way I could back down. I knew that nothing anybody could do came anywhere close to where I had been. I had absolutely nothing to lose. Carlos Castaneda's words summarized my stance when he said, "A warrior fights every battle as if it is his last."

To everyone's amazement, I went to work and stood up to the big man who had given me so much grief. I spoke my mind and set him straight about right and wrong and how to treat people. I told him he had better damned well respect me because I worked hard to accomplish what I had and I not only deserved respect; I demanded it.

To make a long story short, he gave me a 21 percent raise and a manager's position. I didn't care about job, money, life, or anything. I knew I was right, and that was all that mattered. I felt pure abandon, and I felt power, especially from the respect that came from those around me and the awe from them at what I had done. I first thought of my breakdown as an exorcism because I felt cleaner and lighter as a result of it, but I now understand it as the boundary between my shadow self and the face I showed to the world dissolving, causing my dark side to rise up and swallow me. In my nothing-to-lose moment, when I confronted my big boss and demanded my respect, I not only felt fearless, but I also felt totally free.

Things in my life picked up. What I learned in my moment of darkness gave me power, a deeper respect for others, and the opening of a new blossom. My increased empathy complemented my intuition, my sense of people, and my sense of where they really lived.

It showed me their hearts.

III

BLOSSOM

THIRTY-NINE

The Blossom Unfolds

I experienced my first transformation at the age of twenty-one when I had my cosmic flash after ingesting thirteen Hawaiian baby woodrose seeds on the day of the summer solstice. Twenty-one years later, at the age of forty-two, I unwittingly had a second life-changing transformation on the day of the spring equinox, once more ingesting thirteen Hawaiian baby woodrose seeds; this time combining them with what Terence McKenna would call a "heroic dose" of nine grams of mushrooms that nearly killed me. I had consciously and unconsciously pushed the envelope out of a drive to escape a reality I no longer felt compatible with, but my efforts backfired and my dark, shadow side that I tried to escape lured me into its open and waiting maw. Having survived, I reaped the benefits of the explosive expansion of consciousness I experienced in its wake. My journey to hell turned out to be one of the best things that had ever happened to me, and I am deeply thankful that I passed through my dark night of the soul graced by the Great Spirit to live to tell about it.

A multitude of revelations cascaded in destroying what I had been, while germinating what I was to become. Going to hell meant annihilating my ego, and its dissolution brought the experience of sacrifice, death, and rebirth in the form of a classic shamanic dismemberment. The pain brought with it a force more powerful than anything I could imagine short of death, saturating me with a deep understanding of the evolution of consciousness, something that would be reinforced with increasing clarity in future visions. The process of my rebirth taught me how consciousness evolves, beginning with single-celled organisms. These basic units of life have awareness of themselves and their primitive life functions of nourishment and reproduction wherein the cell absorbs its food and splits in two to reproduce. These individuals evolve into loosely based colonies, representing primal group consciousness that share an environment conducive to their life's continuation. At this basic level, the cells are autonomous, not needing any help, nurturing, or interaction with others of their kind. They only need themselves for reproduction.

Taking the next step up the evolutionary ladder, colonies of organisms grow and work together for the common goal of species propagation, shared nourishment, and shared environment. Bigger leaps and bounds up the ladder bring smaller plants and insects, and cells give up their individuality to perform more specific functions. Root cells agree to be root cells and leaf cells performing photosynthesis agree to be leaf cells. If cells didn't diversify, higher organisms such as blades of grass would not exist.

In the same way, visual, olfactory, and other specialized cells of insects must be individuated to perform their specific functions or the higher organism could not exist. *Cells that give up their "individuality" gain a higher awareness needed to function as part of a greater whole, and they gain more individuality by their unique talents needed to perform specific functions.* The result is a more highly evolved form of conscious life with a higher level of awareness. In the intelligent plant kingdom, they bend, turn, and grow in places that give them the most beneficial exposure to the proper levels of sun and water conducive to their species. The intelligence of insects is self-evident by their behaviors.

If you follow this paradigm up through increasing levels of complexity in plants, higher animals, and mammals, you have increasing specialization coupled with higher and higher awareness until you reach human beings, the most complex and sophisticated group-consciousness life form on the planet. Humans are an aggregate of a mind-boggling array of approximately fifty trillion unique, individual, specialized cells, with a reflective self-consciousness that makes us uniquely human.

The whole *is* greater than the sum of its parts.

Taking the logical expansion of this paradigm beyond its physical boundaries, this ability to know the self burgeons into the realms of the transpersonal, including mystical experience, telepathy, synchronicity, lucid dreaming, intuition, remote viewing, and all manner of psychic phenomena falling under Jung's model of the collective unconscious. The portal beyond physical boundaries leads to dynamic, multifaceted, archetypal geometric symbolism and other higher forms of expansive language too abstract and esoteric to be constricted by the serial nature of simple words and sentences, the same way that plants teach and speak to the mind in visionary states. Life on earth and the highly intelligent, vastly complex, interdependent interactions of the life forms that coexist within it would not be possible without the plants, who preceded most other life on this planet.

Is it farfetched to believe that our seemingly silent companions, who have been living on this earth longer than we have, could know some things that we don't? Is it possible that something characterized as "dumb as a houseplant" could indeed have something to teach us?

If we could get out of our own egotistical way, we might open ourselves to the awe and wonder of multifaceted, archetypal knowledge that is too abstract and esoteric to be understood within the serial nature of simple words and sentences.

FORTY

Dissolution

I spent the next two months assimilating all the new information that flooded into me after my psychospiritual death and rebirth. The knowledge gained in my spiral through hell left me humbled, with a deep respect for the power of the plants and their ability to catalyze profound transformation. After my night of darkness, I steered clear of visionary experiences and went through my tasks at work as if moving by remote control, feeling blessed with the simple miracle of awakening each morning, filled with newfound clarity and wonder. Events that I had set in motion months before loomed on my horizon, specifically my agreement with Jacques to smoke 5MEODMT together. The way things unfolded, an upcoming Memorial Day weekend provided the best opportunity for us to meet, a short two months after my crash. I felt both terrified and reluctant to embrace a new visionary experience that soon, but Jacques and I had agreed to work together ahead of time and I remained determined to honor our commitment. I met him late Sunday afternoon and we embarked on a mild journey from a Mimosa and Syrian Rue concoction we had brewed as an ayahuasca analog. After a night's sleep and a morning of reconnecting, we came to our moment of truth and the real reason we had come together.

We examined the white powder I had purchased by mail, smelled it, and tried to figure out the best way to calculate a dose and smoke it. Sprinkling it over cannabis seemed like the most efficient method. Since I had purchased the 5MEO and initiated our meeting, we decided that I would try it first.

I approached my first hit with great respect and a healthy level of trepidation, evident by my sweaty palms and jittery stomach, but I tempered my fear with resolve. I had never smoked DMT, but I had experienced every imaginable LSD experience a hallucinating twentieth century man could conjure, yet none of my scares or bum trips came close to the terror of my fall into hell, which now loomed heavy in my heart. After breathing deeply and centering myself, I took what I thought to be a healthy bong hit of 5MEO sprinkled over a small bed of cannabis, but I felt nothing more than a sense of heaviness.

"I don't know," I said to Jacques. "Maybe getting something like this legally through the mail is too good to be true."

"I heard sometimes it takes a second hit," he said, gently encouraging me.

I loaded up the bong with a little more and took a second hit. I felt more of the heaviness but nothing more.

"This is bullshit," I said. "I think we got ripped off. I wasn't so sure about getting this stuff through the mail."

"Sometimes, I heard, it takes a third hit," Jacques said, still not ready to give up.

I looked at him and weighed things through in my mind, then said, "Third hit, huh? Fuck it!"

I dumped a much bigger pile of 5MEO on top of the cannabis, took a solid third hit and instantly fuzzed out and dissolved the same way I had as a kid when I hyperventilated and passed out. *Oh shit!* I thought as the terror came and annihilated me. In those first moments of being swallowed and flooded by an infinite number of things, I felt my concept of the expansion and evolution of consciousness instantly confirmed before I dissolved into nothingness. I have no idea of how long I was gone. In my first glimmer of returning awareness, it came as a shock to me that I not only experienced the annihilation of everything I knew by becoming both everything and nothing, but I also survived it. In the midst of my receding awe and terror, I knew I had received a gift of power that I had earned by putting myself on the line by my explorations, which amounted to asking questions. I experienced death again in response to this inquiry when I dissolved, embracing the ultimate thrill.

Over time I came to understand that the speed and power of 5MEO caught my ego off guard, and without its hold I was able to give up my *self* and merge with the oneness and trust in perfection. Total surrender to a power greater than yourself is a sacrifice of *self*, a shift from selfishness to selflessness. Total surrender is also the essence of unconditional love. The more you let go and shut off your inner intellectual chatter, the more you receive. This is not only the key to 5MEO; it applies to visionary experience and the learning process in general. Rationality is highly overrated.

Initially I couldn't remember much about my experience, but I had the strangest feeling when I returned. Jacques plucked a string on his guitar, bringing me back to the here and now, only it didn't feel like returning to this reality. It felt turned around, as if reality had gone and now returned to me. He told me I had been moving around, talking and gesturing with my eyes open during my experience, but I had no memory of it. Once I felt grounded, we had a better idea of gauging an effective dose, so we prepared the bong for Jacques. I could sense the power and intensity of my own journey in the way Jacques readied himself with deep breathing, centering, and a blessing to himself. I also saw his fear and resolve when he took his hit.

He laid back and closed his eyes while I watched his breathing closely. His eyes jittered back and forth in a frantic REM state. Then he sat straight up with his eyes bugged out of his head and let out one of the most terrifying scream I have ever heard—a truly primal one. Hoping the neighbors didn't hear, I went to his side and comforted him with words and gentle strokes until he fell silent. His scream was one of the eeriest things I have ever witnessed, reinforced by the look of pure terror in his widened eyes.

When I asked him about it afterward, he smiled and said that he could only remember bliss. I have no doubt that his mind blocked out the terror. It explained why I couldn't remember much of anything myself. I knew that Jacques screamed when the lid blew off of his subconscious, exposing all the fears and demons that had been bottled up there.

My experience kept coming back to me in my dreams with increasing frequency until I found my awareness dancing on the edge of an abyss, knowing that if I went into it I would dissolve. The fear of not coming back remained strong and stayed with me for months. Finally I found myself in that shadowy place somewhere between waking, sleeping, and dreaming, at the edge of the abyss in mortal terror until the thought struck me that if I had already died many times over, what was I afraid of?

With that thought I slipped into the abyss and dissolved, ceasing to exist for an indefinite period of time until I bubbled back into awareness again, pleasantly surprised. I dissolved and returned again and again, marveling at the novelty of the whole experience until I came to love what I had feared very much. With this conquering of my fear, my mind began reintegrating the parts of my experience that I had been too awestruck and terrified to remember.

In the days and weeks that followed, Jacques and I had many discussions during which the two of us worked together to come to terms with what we had experienced. We both felt that our grasp of reality had been unhinged in a most exquisite way and we both felt disoriented, as though our former concept of ourselves had been bulldozed. In its place came new insights and conceptions of the nature of reality and our place within it.

Only one word can truly describe our experience.

Ineffable.

In our loss of self, we experienced awe, ecstasy, and rapture, manifesting in an overwhelming flood of pleasure, love, and terror. The concept of a huge thrill only hints at its nature and intensity. Our physical boundaries fell away and we became the essence of our beings, literally swallowed up in creation by becoming one with it in pure awareness before returning once more to the physical. I can't articulate how good it felt to see Jacques on my return and how thankful I felt to have him there dancing on the edge with me. Our shared experience gave us an incredibly deep sense of brotherhood.

My fall into hell enlivened my spirit and set into motion a process of ego dissolution and reintegration that 5MEO compounded and amplified. My ego death and rebirth sparked an ongoing cycle that continues to enlighten and expand me with a multitude of new and increasingly complex interconnected insights.

FORTY-ONE

Brave New World

he reintegration that started after my passage through hell quickened after my 5MEO experience and continued to unfold in the months that followed, restructuring my whole view of reality and my place in it. I often returned to the experience in my dreams, or more accurately, the experience returned to me. In brief instances I found myself dissolving, which unnerved me, especially with other people around. I soon realized that though these episodes felt subjectively long to me, in real time they came as brief flashes that no one ever noticed. Time and again I fell into deep reveries, puzzling over the process happening inside of me, feeling as if hardly anybody on the planet had a clue about what the universe really consisted of.

What I had first feared became a novelty, and I began to understand that these flashes showed me that my perspective had become un-tethered in a most exquisite way. My new detachment fell along the lines of what I had read in the books of Carlos Castaneda. In my universe my assemblage point had broken free, meaning I had lost my narrow lock on "consensual reality."

I danced around the edges of smoking 5MEO again, but other than Jacques, I didn't know anybody I could trust to understand and sit for me, so I continued assimilating my experience, marveling at its profound, life-changing, and powerfully expansive impact. I wondered how it would be to experience it again with the knowledge gained from my first egress. Could it be any better? The same? More centering? I thought about it frequently, but I wasn't sure I had the nerve to do it again.

After nine months of coming to terms with my first experience, I attended a second entheobotany seminar near the Maya ruins of Palenque. Once more I found myself blessed to spend the week with Terence McKenna and the other knowledgeable souls I had connected with. I didn't know that this would be the last time I would see Terence. A few months after the conference, he was diagnosed with a brain tumor that quickly ended his life.

I gathered my nerve again while down in Palenque, and with a group of supportive people who I had shepherded through the experience, I took my second 5MEO plunge. This time the fear evaporated and I immersed myself in the oneness, feeling protected by the love of those who watched over me. With my fall into hell triggering the profound changes I experienced, did I dare think that I experienced death in the shamanic tradition and had undergone some kind of personal shamanic transformation, or was I just crazy, drugged out, and deluded?

This thought filled my mind the same way the question did when the rainbow came as an answer to my concerns at the Magician's Pyramid in Uxmal, only this time the answer came the way my altar had presented itself to me in my living room. On the way to the conference, I read the first half of Wade Davis's book, *Shadows in the Sun*. On the plane home, I dropped into my seat and flipped open to the page I was about to read in it, once more experiencing astonishment upon reading the first words of page 145.

"For unlike the priest, who is a socially inducted and initiated member of a recognized religious organization, the shaman is one who, as a consequence of a completely personal psychological crisis, has gained a certain power of his or her own. Whereas the priest is concerned with integrating the individual into a firmly ordered and well-established social context, the shaman seeks the release of his or her own wild genius, wherever that may lead. Almost invariably, an overwhelming mental crisis is part of the vocational summons. Indeed, for the seeker of shamanic wisdom, it is a fine line between mystical initiation and psychological breakdown.

Yet, though this crisis may resemble a mental breakdown, it cannot be dismissed as one. For it is not a pathological but a normal event for the gifted mind in these societies, the realization and intuition of a level of spiritual depth that gives the world a sacred character. By following the solitary vision, the shaman breaks not with the other traditions of his tribe but with the comparatively trivial attitude toward the spirit realm that seems to satisfy the majority. In seeking this most difficult path, the shaman becomes a master of death and resurrection, of health and well-being."

This is exactly what happened to me, although I had no inkling of it in my moments of darkness. I don't consider myself gifted or a genius, but I do feel blessed to be alive, especially at this most exciting time in the history of the earth. As a result of these revelations and my experiences, I felt as if I lived even more in the moment than ever before, marveling at the way my glimpse of the other side brought such profound changes. My life moments multiplied in intensity and I gained a stronger sense of well-being, as if my soul had opened like a burgeoning blossom, more fully embracing the reality I inhabit. All of my senses and sensibilities felt like their volume had been turned up.

I felt empowered with new confidence that I could do anything I wished in this mysterious world we live in. I started working toward lucid dreams again after a twenty-year hiatus. Everything I did in my life felt imbued with power. My synchronicities also increased along with my intuition and psychic awareness. I often knew who was calling when the phone rang and found myself thinking of someone only to have them appear at the door in the next moment. I found my nonstop, dynamic, ongoing re-assimilation to be most remarkable. After Palenque I did 5MEO many times and guided dozens of people on their journeys. Most of them had peaceful, blissful experiences, but every so often, someone went through the experience of howling or screaming in terror. I believe that these people were reliving their birth traumas.

I continued working at my job and kept at my writing, only now I did it from a different perspective. I felt free enough to walk away from everything at a moment's notice, which felt exceptionally empowering, but I knew I had people to awaken, so I kept on my path with my heart and mind open, ready to embrace whatever came my way. I considered 5MEO to be a sacrament and one of the greatest gifts that I could give a person. Its experience is one of the most sacred life has to offer, but only if a person is ready to receive it, and only if it is used with the utmost integrity, reverence, and respect.

Misusing it carries great consequences, and it is not for the faint of heart.

FORTY-TWO

Holographic Integration

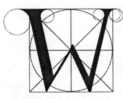hen the bigger pieces of my life's puzzle integrated in the months that followed, I gained a more complete understanding of what had occurred. My subjective, precipitous drop into hell came from my shadow rising up full force from the depths of my repressed subconscious to swallow me whole. By relentlessly pushing the envelope, I had broken the subconscious barrier, letting my demons loose from their cage to run rampant, temporarily taking me over and pulling me down into the darkness they had been imprisoned in for God knows how long.

In my fumbling for more understanding, I stumbled into a process that opened many doorways within me. Terror waited behind more than I cared to take on, but behind that overwhelming horror, on the other side of my darkest fears, wonderful gifts of wisdom and the tools for a dawning inner peace awaited.

eobotany seminars in Palenque, I had the honor of
d Sasha Shulgin, the authors of *Thikal* and *Phikal*. Anne
sychotherapist and Sasha is a brilliant chemist who is
grandfather of designer drugs. Anne encouraged me to
void experience and further sparked the research my
intellect craved to connect the dots from my firsthand experience with
the darkness. I soon learned that the process I had semi-consciously
initiated is called individuation, based on a term coined by Carl Jung.
When we are born into this world, we bring with us the positive and
negative impulses and behaviors that make us human. As we grow into
individuals, those aspects of our self that are considered unacceptable—
whether dictated by the mores of society, family, church, school,
environment, or any other factors—are repressed and soon forgotten;
or so we'd like to think.

Shadow work entails tracking down these hidden aspects of ourselves
and reintegrating them back into our core selves to become whole,
once again owning and acknowledging all of our lost and abandoned
parts. The goal is wholeness, not perfection. Each of these fragmented
selves became suppressed from traumas that gave us the message that
some part of us was unacceptable.

A toddler innocently expressing an artistic impulse could scribble
all over the walls with a crayon and be punished for making a mess. In
their confusion, the toddler may relate the artistic impulse to something
bad and spend the rest of their life with an aversion to artistic self-
expression, thinking it unacceptable. The pain of the initial trauma is
the first wound, and each successive emotion that engenders the same
feeling builds on this original trauma, covering it with layer after layer
of energetic reinforcement, obscuring the original wound until it is no
longer recognizable.

From a shamanic perspective, everything is energy and trauma is
stored energetic patterns representing splintered aspects of yourself.
Shamans call it soul retrieval when they recover an individual who
has been shut away in the darkness for a lifetime. When the fragment
is rediscovered, it is both angry and terrified at being abandoned.
When it is re-embraced, the original trauma is relived with the added
perspective of a mature, objective witness. While someone is reliving
and reacceptance, the energy that kept the "demon" caged is released

to the individual and reintegrated, making them more whole, more balanced, and gradually over time, more at peace with "them selves." When liberated, each of these demons brings the gift of themselves for your higher self. In the case of someone artistically challenged, their creativity can become unleashed in ways never before imagined because of the dissolution of the fear that kept it stuffed. Multiple personalities are extreme cases of shattering and splintering from traumas so untenable that distinct personalities become clearly apparent as mechanisms to cope with what we think of as unacceptable.

In denying our shadow selves, we not only deny our wholeness; in their desperation to be heard, the negative parts of us that we consciously and unconsciously deny existence sneak out when we are not fully aware and we project our faults onto others. In truth, it is the things that we judge and harshly criticize others for that we hide and deny the most in ourselves. When we come to terms with our own demons based on some form of greed, self-deprecation, impatience, arrogance, martyrdom, self-destruction, or stubbornness, we not only embrace and heal them in ourselves; we contribute to the healing of the whole. In our own firsthand experience of forgiving and acknowledging these behaviors in ourselves, we gain compassion when we see them in others.

In the eyes of shamans, the all-encompassing energy of spirit makes up and interconnects reality. Everything is contained in the whole and the whole is contained in everything. Quantum physics has shown that if an atom is split and its electrons spin off in opposite directions, altering the spin of one of the electrons, *regardless of time or distance from the split, causes the other electron to respond with a corresponding alteration in its spin.* The oneness and interconnectedness of all that manifests as the whole within all of the parts is the definition of a holograph, which is the form that the universe takes on all of its levels.

In the physical world, holographs are those shiny mirrored, rainbow colored images that have become commonplace on credit cards. To create one, a laser beam is split into two separate beams. The first beam is bounced off the object that is to be made into a holograph, and the second beam is allowed to collide with the reflected light of the first. The resulting interference pattern is recorded onto film, making a three-dimensional image of the original object that appears within the interference pattern. Aside from its ghostly three dimensional image, if you divide a holograph into increasingly smaller and smaller pieces, *the whole image is contained in all of the smaller parts.* There does come a point where the pieces are so small that the resolution drops out, but the principle remains.

We are holographic by our very nature. We are the center of the universe. We are human beings: hue-man, meaning "light-man beings." We are the manifestation of an interference pattern that is a self-conscious point where spirit meets matter and subject meets object. Each of our senses operates by an objective, subjective interference pattern that combines to create reality as we know it.

Our divided selves are holographic, ghostly images of our whole selves stored within specific constellations of memories from different periods in our lives that have themes accompanied by strong emotional charges of the same quality, all going back to our biological birth and the experiences of the perinatal period. Stanislav Grof, MD, a leading psychotherapeutic researcher, classified these constellations as systems of condensed experience, which he named COEX.

Every one we encounter are holographs like ourselves, each containing the whole of the universe within. When we do something negative and project our faults onto others for what we ourselves are doing and judge and criticize those others, we are hiding and denying those very qualities within ourselves.

Once I discovered this on a deep non-rational, conceptual, holographic level, the universe, made manifest in my awareness, began to consciously and unconsciously expand in a magical, energetic blossom that continues to encompass more of each moment of my life. This expansion allows me to live more in the moment, bringing with it a broader, increasingly sophisticated perception of the reality that I live within.

FORTY-THREE

Ayahuasca

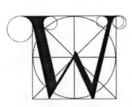ith my new awareness came increased possibilities and more lessons from my developing inner life. Determined to live every moment as if it were my last, I took steps to publish a novel I had written about an eighteenth-century South American shaman caught in the middle of a clash between two cultures; one of them supposedly civilized, the other supposedly primitive. On the one hand, I landed a gifted, loving, and supportive small publisher. On the other, I found myself cursed by an incompetent, unethical publicist who abandoned me when I needed her the most. The book fell short of my financial expectations, but the lessons I learned from the pain of the experience made it all worthwhile.

During the prepublication phase of my novel's release, I wrangled an invitation to drink what many believe to be the highest of all plant teachers, ayahuasca. When I told my publisher and her husband about it, to my amazement, they asked me if I would take their son, a young man in his early twenties.

I took him to the gathering against my better judgment, thinking it would be an ayahuasca circle, but instead of an ayahuasca circle, our host called our group a symposium, which consisted of eighteen people gathered in a circle in a big hall for an all-night session where each person would take something different. Some took mushrooms, others Iboga; and a few took ayahuasca while the rest took San Pedro, LSD, or some combination of substances. I had just started feeling the effects of the bitter molasses-like ayahuasca when my young friend started babbling nonsensically. He ignored or couldn't hear any efforts to quiet him and grew louder and increasingly disruptive to the point that we had to take him out of the circle. I felt responsible because I had brought him, so I spent the better part of the night babysitting him while on ayahuasca myself, separate from the rest of the circle. I had gotten high on the ayahuasca, but the sobering immediacy of my responsibility kept me from my journey. When we left the next day, I thought I would never be invited back.

My publisher called one day, telling me that my novel had come in from the printer, so I left work early and went to her house for a celebration lunch and an official box-opening ceremony. After our celebration I buzzed home with a box of books, excited that my years of hard work had finally become a reality. My phone rang around ten o'clock that night. I picked it up and heard Jacques telling me that he was getting ready for the AllChemical Arts Conference in Hawaii, a week-long conference about the interplay of psychedelic substances and creativity. Since Palenque, Terence McKenna had been diagnosed with an inoperable brain tumor. We all knew he would be at this conference, which would most likely be his last. Because of my magical connection with him, I wanted him to get a copy of my novel before he passed on. I had put him in its dedication with the other people who had inspired me and passed on, and I felt self-conscious about it until I realized that Terence of all people would understand and appreciate the irony.

Jacques planned to stay up all night packing to leave for Hawaii in the morning, and he agreed to personally deliver my book to Terence. I thought it appropriate that my soul-exploring brother would be the one to put my book in Terence's hands, so I made up a care package for Terence and gave him the very first copy of my book from its first printing, signed to him. I left home at ten thirty that night to drive the two and a half hours to Jacques' house, where I stayed for a couple of hours. Then I turned around and drove back, returning home at six that morning. I hit the shower, started drinking coffee, and went in to work, putting in a full day before collapsing into bed that following night.

To my joy and amazement, a few weeks prior to my book's official publication, I received an invitation to a full-on ayahuasca circle, presided over by a shaman from the Amazon called an *ayahuasquero*, who specialized not only in ayahuasca but in the usage of many other healing plants. I couldn't wait.

The magical healing potion known as ayahuasca has been used throughout the jungles of South America since prehistoric times. It is primarily a mixture of two plants, though other helper plants are occasionally added to the brew. The ayahuasca vine used in the brew that carries its name is classified as Banisteriopsis caapi, also known as the vine of death, the vine of the soul, caapi, yajé, and many other names. Though it contains trace amounts of dimethyltryptamine and 5MEODMT, the ayahuasca vine is not the primary psychoactive component of the brew. Another plant called chacruna, classified as Psychotria viridis, contains the psychoactive DMT component. Taken orally by itself, the stomach's monoamine oxidase, or MAO enzymes, digest the DMT in the chacruna before it can cross the blood-brain barrier. Adding the ayahuasca vine with its beta carbolines to the DMT-loaded chacruna leaves provides an MAO inhibitor to the stomach, making the DMT in the chacruna orally active, which produces the profound and startling experiences that the ayahuasca brew brings.

One of the amazing mysteries about the history of the brew is how humans from prehistoric times came across such a unique combination of two plants that produces such remarkable psychoactive properties out of the thousands of choices available in the rich biodiversity of the Amazon rain forest. If you ask a shaman about its discovery, he will tell you that the plants themselves told him how to mix them.

A legend from the Shipibo Indians, a vanishing Amazonian tribe steeped in ayahuasca lore, tells the story of a woman who bathed herself every day with chacruna leaves down by the waters of a river. One day the spirit of the chacruna plant came to her and asked her why she bathed herself with its leaves. She said that she liked their smell and the way they made her feel. The spirit of the chacruna plant told her to mix the leaves with the vines of the ayahuasca plant to make the brew and introduce the world to the spiritual wisdom of the plant teacher, considered by Amazonian shamans to be the "mother of all the plants."

Regardless of the shadowy origins of this mystical, life-changing concoction, its history and usage are mind-boggling when you consider the sophistication contained in the knowledge of biochemistry and physiology necessary to produce its psychoactive effects. This brilliant neurochemistry comes from people the Western world, in its superstition and ethnocentricity, have always considered to be primitive savages.

Out of respect for this plant teacher, I had to follow a cleansing diet for a week prior to drinking it, which meant no oils, dairy, salt, spicy foods, citrus, acids like tomatoes, pork, red meat, caffeine, drugs, alcohol, or stimulants of any kind, and no excessively hot or cold food or drinks. I could only eat bland, basic protein and carbohydrates. They told me that the cleaner and less toxic I could be going in, the better the experience would be.

I left early on the day of the session to give myself plenty of time to prepare. Two other people had arrived before me, a soon-to-be husband and wife named Lorenzo and Mary Kay. Lorenzo, an older long-haired hippie, and I hit it off immediately. A writer himself with a technical background similar to mine, Lorenzo had unbounded enthusiasm for life, especially writing. As we talked I offered to show him and Mary Kay my book. We went to the car, and as I opened the trunk, they started talking about a book Terence had with him at the AllChemical Arts Conference, where they had just been. They told me that Terence had carried this book with him during the whole conference and read it every chance he could. They wanted to know who wrote it because they wanted to get it and read it. Their mouths dropped when I took my book from the trunk. "That's it!" they said.

A surge of happiness passed through me and a connection completed between me, Lorenzo, and Mary Kay; a synchronistic moment that came because of our unique connections to Terence.

Other people started arriving until fifteen of us filled the big room, all situated in a circle with a place for the shaman at the head of it. Once settled, our host introduced a short, husky, dark-haired ayahuasquero from the Amazon named José. Before the session started, José donned a white intricately patterned robe and a pillbox-style hat.

We each drank a shot glass full of a thick, molasses-like, bitter brew, turned out all the lights, and waited while José sang softly, sometimes whistling, sometimes whispering in what I can only describe as an exquisite fashion. I waited in anticipation, remembering what someone had told me: ayahuasca is the river and the magical songs and chants called *icaros* and *mariris* that the shaman sings are the boats that transport you along it to other dimensions.

I experienced this firsthand from José, who sang, played a flute, whistled, and strummed a sweet-sounding mandolin-like instrument from Peru called a charango. José's combinations of celestial sound and music took me through a succession of experiences and places that defy logic. Many strange, otherworldly perceptions came to me that night. I remember looking again and again at the head of the circle where José sat. I could make out the forms of the others, but José's spot looked like a nonexistent void where he should have been.

Where is José? I wondered. In that moment I felt him everywhere throughout the room, as if his awareness had scattered itself and existed both everywhere and nowhere. Amid a flood of visions, I became Ganesha, the Hindu god of wisdom and patron of sciences, arts, and creative activities, an elephant-headed man representing the microcosm and the macrocosm. The elephant head symbolizes the human potential to become enlightened. Then I transformed into a human roman candle, spewing ecstatic, joy-filled, colored balls of energy into the sky that took the forms of sacred geometry unfolding in dynamic, multicolored, holographic, geometric progressions that taught me the nature of blossoming macroscopic and microscopic life, genetic expression, and the expansion of consciousness in the molecular, human, planetary, and galactic realms. At one point I became lost in a drumming revelry until I was asked to quiet down. I caught myself and looked around to see most if not all of the others in the group moaning and vomiting. I hadn't even been aware of the fact that everyone else wasn't having the ecstatic time of their life, like me.

Ineffable, sublime, and exquisite are half-hearted attempts to define by serializing what is nonlinear, non-rational, and multidimensional by nature. I often felt myself swept backward and forward in time, space, and strange dimensions, sometimes inhabited by even stranger beings. I learned volumes that night in an abstract and symbolic language that spoke in dynamic holograms, or what Terence McKenna called "self-transforming machine elves." When the energy of the circle diminished, José formally closed it and made the rounds, checking up on everyone. When he came to me, he squatted down in front of me, and with a huge grin on his face, said in Spanish accented English, "The mother *loves* you."

All I could think of was *Wow!*

Later that night, after things quieted, I lay awake outside, stretched out on a picnic table. I could swear I heard José's voice whispering through the branches of the trees, but I felt no wind.

Lorenzo and Mary Kay married and came to my publication party, which turned out to be an amazing event where all of my worlds crossed, bringing together family, writing, shamanism, work, and other improbable associations.

While there, Lorenzo told me, "I've decided that I'm going to call you Cassouac."

Cassouac? I thought, puzzled. "Sounds pretty cool. Like an Indian."

"You are a manic, frenzied, free spirit like Neil Cassidy, and you're a writer like Jack Kerouac, so you're Cassouac."

He told this to my mother and she said, "He's a better writer than Kerouac."

I felt honored that Lorenzo gave me this name, and he continued to call me it until it stuck. For those who don't know, Neil Cassidy was the model for the main character—the amped-out speed-freak driver—in Jack Kerouac's *On The Road*, a book considered by many to be the voice of the beat generation. Cassidy also drove the bus named Furthur that took Ken Kesey's Merry Pranksters and their Electric Kool-Aid Acid Test cross country to turn on as many people as possible to LSD.

Both roles had been shamanic in that they created a bridge between generations from the beats to the hippies, then from the hippies beyond. Each cross-country ride—first in a car for the beats, then in a bus for the hippies—manifested as agents on the cutting edge of deep cultural change unlike anything the Western world had seen.

I attended the Palenque Entheobotany conference with Lorenzo and Mary Kay in the beginning of 2000, and we "created our own legend," as Lorenzo put it. Through him and Mary Kay, I met more brothers and sisters of the tribe who lived close to me. Terence couldn't come because his health had declined dramatically and he was nearing death. In his absence the conference took on a super-charged, frenetic energy, giving everyone a peak experience in what may have been the best conference ever. The energy reached such heights that it felt as if Terence's missing physical presence manifested itself in the spirits of all who attended.

We all knew that if it hadn't been for Terence, most of us would not have come to the tribe.

FORTY-FOUR

The Call of the Wild

I now understood on deeper levels that reality in its infinite permutations is composed of energy, meaning everything we think, perceive, or imagine is composed of energy. Reality's slower three-dimensional vibrations exhibit the phenomena of duration and persistence, creating the illusion of permanence, but in truth everything is transitory. I believe that ayahuasca shifts the frequency of a person's consciousness into their energetic spirit body. In an ayahuasca session, music and sound, being expressions of energy themselves, give the energetic body a homing signal to tune into. In the same way that a radio tunes into a particular station, our holographic mind tunes to the frequencies of times, places, and other dimensions through the medium of the music. When our mind resonates with them, it tunes into their time-space coordinates and manifests within them. The landscapes you experience in an ayahuasca session cleanse you physically, psychically, and spiritually. In its enhancement of the shadow work and individuation process, ayahuasca seeks out your fears and traumas and exploits them in direct proportion to the level they are present in you. When you confront a particularly strong trauma, stored as an energetic pattern, you often vomit forcefully. You may also experience powerful bowel movements. On the physical level, these provide deep physical cleansing to your digestive tract. Ayahuasca also contains powerful anti-parasitic properties. The possibilities of puking and shitting turn the faint of heart away from this potent plant medicine, but in these reactions you expel poisons, not only physically but psychically as well, by clearing yourself out on deep energetic levels.

Ayahuasqueros also call ayahuasca *"La purga,"* the purge. Each time I have vomited, it had a slingshot effect, and the harder I purged, the more sublime and exquisite the realms I found myself transported to in the aftermath. Ayahuasca takes you to the upper, lower, and middle worlds so you can experience them all. Some sessions are blissful, some hellish, and some a combination of both; bouncing between the agony and the ecstasy. Whether your experiences are light, dark, or both, you *always* learn and you *always* benefit, whether freed from traumas or taught, enlightened, and entertained. The transformative process stays with you, continuing in the days and weeks that follow, sometimes coming to you in your dreams and in day-to-day revelations.

A few months after my first ayahuasca circle, I took my second journey and still didn't vomit. I drank ayahuasca on a dozen separate occasions before I did vomit. Then it seemed like I did nothing but vomit for the next dozen. In my second session and the few that followed, I rediscovered my feminine side after spending my life as a macho hardass.

On that dark night when I fell into hell, I cried for the first time in thirty years, crying so hard that my throat stayed sore for a week. Under the teaching of ayahuasca over the course of a few circles, I cried more, each time accepting more of my repressed feminine side. It had nothing to do with sexual orientation and everything to do with becoming a more balanced being. The more I accepted the sensitive, feminine side of myself, the more my intuition blossomed, and the greater my compassion and understanding was for women, who had always puzzled me to no end. I also gained a new appreciation for nature, flowers, and all things nurturing and manifesting life that women have a special connection with.

In my visions, ayahuasca continued teaching me on different levels about the nature of cosmic reality through transforming microcosmic and macrocosmic landscapes and synaesthetic, flowing multicolored geometric patterns of sound and color. I also experienced moving forward, backward, and sideways through time and space, often finding myself in the presence of strange alien, insect–like, and reptilian creatures, and a variety of otherworldly beings with different shapes and forms. One of the remarkable things about ayahuasca is that it overwhelms the rational, imprisoning intellectual thought structures that people construct. Most people believe that the consensual reality we know of as waking consciousness is the only form of reality possible. Ayahuasca teaches you differently through experiential learning, something you can never get from a book. It can only be gained through firsthand experience.

Ayahuasca visions begin with increasing speed and a density of information that is so fast and immense that the rational mind is overwhelmed. When people identify too much with their rational mind, this influx of information is awesome, terrifying, and incomprehensible. Once they learn to surrender, flow, and accept what is happening without trying to rationalize everything, they learn to "dance with the lady" and "download" the experience in a more direct manner, through the heart. As long as their ego babbles away, they expend their energy outward, canceling out a good portion of the fullness they could be receiving if they could simply shut up and pay attention with all of their being, especially their heart. You cannot receive if you are continually transmitting.

Ayahuasca teaches in symbolism that contains condensed meaning in forms that follow the laws of sacred geometry. This communication is superior to spoken and written language, which is serial, meaning that the message can only come out in a string, one word at a time. A three-dimensional, holographic, transforming sacred geometric symbol, by its very nature, contains far broader depth and meaning.

The whole is contained in the part.

Witnessing how life manifests from the infinitely macroscopic down to the infinitesimal microcosm and back again provides a firsthand

experience of the nature of reality that connects you all
to the archetypes, which are the most highly condens
manifestations of truth that humans know. When you
your mind and accept the teaching, you integrate the
the days and weeks that follow in an unfolding process during which
your rational mind puts the pieces together in its own time. Much of
the learning of reintegration happens in the dreaming state, where the
rational mind is more accepting of the teachings, because in that state
our rules of reality are more flexible.

With continued work, primarily with ayahuasca but also with other
consciousness altering sacraments, the process of reintegrating your
splintered shadow selves and the resulting expansion of consciousness
proceeds along a multidimensional, holographic axis. This blossoming
follows a progression the same way a single-celled organism does when
it takes its next step up the evolutionary ladder, transforming into
higher consciousness constructs that themselves blossom into higher
and higher levels of transpersonal awareness.

The story of the three little pigs and the big bad wolf provides
the perfect metaphor for this unfolding paradigm of expanding
consciousness. The straw house is a metaphor for the rational mind.
Once this gets blown down by the wolf, which represents a force
stronger than the pigs, they build a wooden house. This too gets blown
down, but the pigs learn from each experience, so the wisdom gained
helps them build the brick house from a new perspective that makes
them safer.

Applying these principles on a more complex level bears out their
truth in a little-known science called cymatics, pioneered by Dr. Hans
Jenny in the twentieth century. Jenny took the fine spores of a mold,
water, and other substances conducive to free movement, put them
on smooth surfaces, and ran sound waves through them. At certain
frequencies and amplitudes the substances formed into dynamic
mandala patterns. When he raised the frequency and amplitude, these
fluid patterns dissolved into chaos. When he continued increasing the
amplitude and frequency, *new, more intricate and sophisticated patterns
formed out of the chaos.*

From a psychological perspective, when your direct experience of
reality overwhelms your preconceived version of the world, your mind

es on more than it can assimilate based on the limited constructs previously held to be true. The knowledge and energy you experience in this visionary state exceeds the limitations of your container, overloading it until it shatters and dissolves into chaos. When your new conception of reality reforms itself, it does so in a more sophisticated pattern that forms out of the chaos.

My first break, dissolution, and shamanic dismemberment came with my fall into hell, setting in motion a dynamic evolving process of expansive learning that followed the patterns I have described. Mostly with ayahuasca but also with 5MEO, mushrooms, LSD, and other sacraments used with conscious intention, this expanding, unfolding, blossoming process of life, death, and rebirth continued at a quickened pace.

After a number of ayahuasca sessions with the *ayahuasqueros*, I was blessed by an invitation to spend ten days with them deep in the Amazon jungle. Under their guidance, I would partake in an intensive ayahuasca *dieta*, working with a combination of healing plants. During my stay in the jungle, I would spend most of my time alone in a hut, meeting every other night with others for a total of five ayahuasca circles.

When this was offered to me, there was no question in my mind. It was something I absolutely had to do.

FORTY-FIVE

Passage into the Wild Frontier

ome time in my mid-twenties, my relationship with my mother shifted from that of mother and son to that of best friends and confidantes. She told everybody she knew that *I* was her best girlfriend because she told me everything. As time passed, I told her pretty much everything I did and, to her shock and amazement, much of what I had done in the past, although I spared her the worst of the darkest details. I didn't want to keep any secrets from her, especially when it came to what I learned and experienced with the plants. When I spoke of them, she always listened with apprehension, but she kept her mind open and asked questions. Her worst impression of them came from the night I took the mushrooms and rosewood seeds and nearly killed myself on my plunge into hell. The last thing in the world I wanted was to scare her the way I had, but that night, in my desperation, she had been the only one in the whole universe I could talk to who might understand.

Though still fearful for me, she expressed interest in ayahuasca when I spoke of it, and she seemed to have an intuitive understanding of the processes it set in motion. In my early work with it, while I was rediscovering my feminine side, the smallest things made me emotional, like when she called to wish me happy birthday one morning. The sound of her voice and the love it radiated sent me blubbering out of control. When I could finally speak to tell her what I felt, she said, "Is this part of the process of what you're learning?" When I told her yes, she told me she understood, and I knew she did.

Her anxiety rose when I decided to go to the Amazon.

"Wait a minute. Do you mean to tell me that you're going into the middle of the jungle to hallucinate?" she asked, incredulously.

"That's right."

"Oh my God."

She was nervous about me going to politically unstable South America and felt scared for my safety in the jungle until she heard a tape of me being interviewed on a radio show about shamanism and visionary experience. Once she heard me on the tape, she realized that I had done a lot of research and I knew what I was talking about. Her fear diminished somewhat, but she still felt uneasy about the thought of me disappearing into the jungle for two weeks, completely out of contact with the rest of the world. I promised her that she would be the first person I would call when I came back to civilization.

I felt apprehensive myself. I had spent a few weeks in Mexico, but my Spanish wasn't very good and I had never been to South America, much less the tropical jungles of the Amazon, yet here I was, "going into the middle of the jungle to hallucinate."

I practiced my Spanish as much as possible and read everything I could about the Amazon, following the ayahuasca diet closely two weeks prior to heading into the jungle. The ten-day *dieta* the shamans planned consisted of a strict plant diet that had its roots in prehistory. The diet contained basic carbohydrates and protein every couple of days in the form of fish and chicken and absolutely no salt. I had been a vegetarian for twenty-three years and had to come to terms with the carnivorous portion of the diet. I trusted the shamans and their ancient knowledge of body chemistry. I wanted to "go native" and do the program in its prehistoric tradition, so I resigned myself to eating chicken and fish and fully embracing the whole experience in the spirit of its original form and intention.

I left the United States with my backpack and a duffel bag full of clothes to give away to people who would need them. We took off on a Friday afternoon, changed planes in Miami around midnight, and arrived in Lima, Peru sometime around four in the morning. Fifteen of us waited eight uncomfortable hours at the Lima airport for the one plane a day that would take us to the jungle town that served as our last "civilized" point of departure on our two-day journey.

I had my first cup of Mate de Coca that morning, a mildly stimulating tea made from coca leaves that is served all over Peru. The tea gently stimulated me, but it had none of the nervous edge and intensity of coffee. Unfortunately coca leaves are the raw material for cocaine, a scourge of the ignorant and ethnocentric war on drugs waged by the government of the United States. The Peruvians don't consider the coca plant to be a drug. Instead they honor it as a sacred plant and have spoken of it with the highest reverence since ancient times, especially in the Andes. Aside from its religious significance, coca combats altitude sickness by increasing the flow of oxygen to the brain. It also has exceptional nutritional value and allows people to work long hours with great energy and minimum food intake. The Peruvians say that refining this sacred plant's essence into cocaine is a sacrilege that shows disrespect for the spirit of the plant. The resulting health problems and addiction are the outcome of this disrespect.

Most Peruvians will tell you, "*Coca no es droga!*"

Fortified by our tea, we boarded our second flight and took off, first flying over the Andes, then over endless green jungle before landing on an old asphalt runway carved out near the edge of the jungle with thatch-roofed huts in various states of disrepair alongside it. Children and adults looked up from their homes to watch us land.

The first thing I felt stepping off the plane was the hot, humid, palpable air that pressed in on us with a presence of its own. Sweat-soaked us as we watched our luggage being loaded onto an old beat-up cart pulled by an ancient tractor, along with a pallet of live chickens. Mestizo and Indian men, women, and children in brightly colored traditional clothes clamored at the terminal exit, offering us cabs and overwhelming us, trying to sell us jewelry and other trinkets. We spotted José in the midst of the crowd with half a dozen battered cabs waiting to whisk us off through overcrowded potholed streets filled with red dust and the hive-like buzzing, smoke, and chaos of two-stroke engines. People zipped in and out of traffic on three-wheeled awning-covered jitney cabs, barely missing each other while obeying few laws but their own, which were enforced by the insistent beeping of their horns. Crowds milled along the sides of the streets and dirt bikes squeezed past us, often carrying father, wife, and two kids all balanced on the seat and gas tank.

We soon arrived at a war-torn-looking "nicer" hotel. Some rooms had half built-walls and no roofs. Barefoot kids and half-starved, mangy dogs ran everywhere. We saw a live deer tied up in the hotel's courtyard with no fence around it. The poverty surrounding us left no doubt that Bambi would probably end up as someone's dinner.

After settling at the hotel, we piled three to a cab into the two-stroke jitneys that buzzed us to a restaurant where we feasted on our last dinner. A delicious grilled Amazon fish called baiche that grows to marlin-sized proportions was the first animal I ate after twenty-three years of abstinence. We ate it with rice, sweet-tasting corn tamales, a salad with avocado, heart of palm, and *chicha*, a sweet, purple-colored corn drink.

I struck up a friendship with a young man named Walter who helped me improve my Spanish while I taught him the finer points of the English language, like the proper use of the words *shit* and *fuck*. He invited me to meet his family that night, which consisted of his mom, dad, five sisters, and a little brother, all sharing what looked and felt like an abandoned gas station off of a dirt road, complete with an old rusting car in the yard, partially inhabited by chickens, with one end of a clothesline tied to it.

Walter's family lived at subsistence level, yet they treated me like royalty, showering me with gifts, including beautiful watercolor pictures painted by his sisters, Shipibo Indian embroidery, and necklaces of seed, bone, claw, and teeth. I particularly treasured a boar's tooth necklace made with seeds that I wore the whole time in the jungle. As an added treat, Walter's sisters played music and sang for me while we all drank Coca-Cola. When the time came for me to leave, I went back to the hotel with Walter and gave him half the contents of my duffle bag for his family in return for the kindness they had shown me.

Our group met later that night after dinner and the shamans laid out the details of the program with the aid of a translator. They planned for us to work primarily with ayahuasca and a second healing plant whose action ties in directly with ayahuasca. We would take this additional plant on a daily basis, with an ayahuasca session every other night, for a total of five group sessions over an eleven-day period. Ayahuasca is always done at night in the dark, but on this program they wanted to do the first session during the day for learning and contrast.

When *ayahuasqueros* talk about an ayahuasca *dieta*, it is not a diet relating to food in the strictest sense; it is also an introspective diet, away from the world and any routines, enmeshed in the fabric of nature. Twice a day they brought us boiled rice, oatmeal, or a grain called *quinoa*, with no spices, salt, or any other additions, along with a baked or boiled, bland, unripe banana called a *plátano* that tastes like cardboard. Every two or three days, we might get a small piece of chicken or fish. A strong pitcher of plant tea made from the second teacher plant would be brought every morning. We had to drink the whole bitter-tasting pitcher during the course of the day.

The intention of the diet is to cleanse and detoxify on all levels and to get in touch with yourself, your environment, and nature in general by becoming integrated with it. To this end, soap, shampoo, toothpaste, bug repellent, deodorant, mouthwash, or any other scents were prohibited. Each morning someone would bring us the crushed leaves of a sweet-smelling plant called huayusa that is similar to eucalyptus yet uniquely different. We were told to mix the crushed leaves with water for a refreshing plant bath that cleansed our physical bodies and our energy fields. The ingested plant diet would clean us from the inside out and the plant bath cleaned us from the outside in.

Over a period of days on this regimen, with nothing to do except be with yourself, the diet, and the ayahuasca sessions every other night, the boundaries between your subconscious and your conscious grow thinner. Because you have no routines, you are often awake half of the night and asleep much of the day. Your dreams grow stronger until the line between waking and dreaming blur. Physically you become weaker while you cleanse the doors of your perception and heighten your awareness. I had no idea what the results of this process would bring, and I was totally unprepared for the depth and nature of what I experienced as a result of it.

FORTY-SIX

Welcome to the Jungle

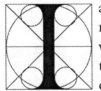ate my first chicken in twenty-three years the following morning in the form of a shredded-chicken sandwich with a glass of papaya juice. After breakfast we navigated through a swarm of Shipibo Indian women and children desperate to sell us jewelry and embroidery as we piled into a line of battered taxis. We left the town behind and drove down dusty, unpaved, sometimes muddy roads full of potholes, passing every vehicle we caught up to, except the other cabs, which took turns flying past each other in heart-quickening maneuvers. Our kamikaze caravan took us through patches of fields and jungle dotted with shacks, broken-down huts, and occasional villages.

After a couple of bone-jarring hours, we came to a village where we became the main attraction. A group of thirty or so kids followed us everywhere. We ate chicken; rice; a lettuce, tomato, and onion salad; and a small potato in a cinderblock structure that smelled of diesel fuel while mangy dogs and baby chickens scrambled around our feet and a wall of kids looked on. Some of the kids sat by us or on our laps, speaking in Spanish and snippets of English. Someone bought a bag of candy and handed it out, and some of us slipped them small change before we went to the river at the edge of town, which served as one of the major tributaries of the Amazon.

Fifteen of us and all of our gear filled two long canoes, each one carved out of a huge tree trunk. Outboard motors with long drive shafts that projected the propeller ten or fifteen feet behind the boats churned bubbling white water some distance behind us and powered us two hours upstream to an unmarked tributary in virgin rain forest where the shaman had a hidden camp. The river rises rapidly with heavy rains and falls slowly when they abate. Our visit coincided with the dry season, when it generally rained every other day instead of every day. The river looked low when we arrived, so we disembarked on the shore of the main river and hiked a half a mile or so through the jungle while smaller canoes navigated the shallow tributary and brought our gear up to the main camp.

Our shirts and pants clung to us, thoroughly soaked from sweat in a matter of minutes while the jungle carried on around us in a cacophony of sight, sound, and scents. Birds, animals, and insects buzzed over the gentle white noise of the water that rose and faded as we moved toward and away from it, while trees, vines, bushes, and strange, sometimes alien-looking plants and beautiful flowers bloomed in the strangest places.

In the rain forest, the bugs eat the plants and feed on the animals who eat the plants, bugs, and other animals. While the big bugs eat the little bugs, the big bugs and the animals die and the little bugs eat them. Anything that is left becomes food for the plants, who feed the bugs and the animals, and of course many of the bugs eat you. One of the primary laws of the jungle is that everything eats everything and you become part of the jungle whether you like it or not.

I learned this firsthand my first day there when they showed us the locations of our individual huts that they called *tambos*. While walking single file along the river trail, Connie, the lady in front of me, started jumping around. As I realized that something had stung her repeatedly, a cloud of wasps swarmed and stung me and most of the others in the same way. Numerous stingers found their way to my stomach, arm, and hand as I slapped away. I learned later that when wasps are killed, they give off a scent that brings more. When the attack subsided, we doubled back the way we had come.

My friend Geramy came running past me with wasps all over his back and stuck in his shirt. My heart went out to him in his helplessness, so I dove into the fray, wrestling his shirt off of his back while wasps stung me up and down my arm, stomach, back, knuckle, and armpit. Geramy wanted to leave his shirt behind, but I felt pissed, so I went back and battled with the remaining living ones that still clung to his shirt. After our escape I made a poultice out of baking soda and applied it to all my stings and the stings of my friends.

While everyone competed for *tambos*, I remained quiet, letting them work out their conflicts. My patience got its reward when I found a *tambo* alongside a stream, back from the tributary, farther away from everyone else, with nothing on the other side of me except jungle. I couldn't hear the rush of the tributary from my spot, only the nonstop buzzing, cries, and calls of bugs and animals.

My open-air *tambo* and the others lining the river each had dirt floors and thatched roofs. All were furnished with a rough hewn table, stool, a small set of shelves, a hammock, and a crude wooden bed built from logs covered with a piece of foam, a sheet, blanket, pillow, and a mosquito net. We each had five gallons of fresh water, a roll of toilet paper, a cigarette lighter, and a small package of candles. This isolated spot would be my home for the next eleven days.

As if reinforcing the jungle's message that everything eats everything, I continued getting lessons and reminders, like when I found my latrine, which consisted of a pit in the ground with a wooden box that had a hole cut in it sitting over the top. Not wanting any surprises, I brushed at its top for spiders but still got bitten in the ass the moment I sat down.

I was drenched with sweat after carrying our gear and getting settled in our *tambos*, so I decided to skinny dip in the tributary. While I was undressing at the water's edge, a huge black ant bit into my foot. I slapped at him, knocking his body away, but his head remained clamped to my foot, still sucking. I swatted it away and still had to dig out its mandibles, which remained embedded in my flesh.

As part of my research, I had read about tiny fish, which are members of the catfish family called candiru, that inhabit parts of the Amazon. These parasitic fish have curved spines that allow them to hook themselves to objects. They obtain their food by eating the gill filaments and drinking the blood of their host. When candiru sense warm water from someone urinating, it is believed that they mistake the flow of human urination for the normal outflow from fish gill openings. Drawn to the warmth, they swim up the hole in the penis or vagina and get lodged by their gills, which act like tiny painful barbs, the same way a fish hook does. They are extremely painful and can require surgery for their removal.

With this knowledge foremost in my mind, I slipped into the refreshing water and in moments, jumped in panic when a number of tiny fish nipped at my bare flesh. To my relief, a guide informed me that these weren't the same fish and they didn't inhabit this part of the Amazon.

Refreshed from my dip, I climbed out of the water and, to my perverse satisfaction and amusement, discovered that when I had brushed one of the huge biting black ants into the river, the ravenous nibbling fish gobbled them in seconds.

Nature does balance things out.

We had our last group dinner that night before going to bed. On the following day, we would break with tradition and have our first ayahuasca session in daylight. During this session the shaman would decide which additional healing plants each of us would be working with. As the day faded, a bird let out a long, shrill cry at six o'clock, which we discovered was a daily ritual. Soon afterward we went off to our *tambos* with further instruction about the meaning of our diet.

In the darkness back at my *tambo*, while preparing for bed, I lit a candle and turned, startled by an ethereal green glow floating toward me. It took a moment before I recognized a firefly lazily buzzing about the forest, something I hadn't seen since childhood. I had never seen one this big. When it landed, its light went out. Two smaller lights at the back of its wings pulsed on and off like a Volkswagen beetle with a pair of glowing tail lights. While I was standing beside my bed in my shorts in the darkness, something big hit my leg, causing me to cry out. Heart slamming in my chest, I grabbed my flashlight and pointed it at the ground to see a huge frog half the size of my head with the legs and wings of what looked like a huge mosquito sticking out of his mouth.

"Thanks, brother," I said, taking deep breaths to calm myself. He stayed there, unfazed by me and my flashlight, and came to be a welcome visitor every night. A short while later, I saw a flashlight bobbing up the creek toward me. Then I saw a young man walking the camp's perimeter with a shotgun, keeping us safe from any disturbances. José had a crew patrolling day and night, watching over us. After he left, I settled in for the night, considering the more in-depth instructions we had received regarding our diet.

The shamanic *dieta* meant a retreat that involved staying out of the sun and away from fire, doing no work, and preparing no food. We had no distractions like radios or fragrances and read only material of a spiritual nature relevant to the experience. We had to conserve our energy on all levels, which meant abstaining from orgasm, keeping contact with others to a minimum, and staying focused inwardly. The purpose in giving up everything is a sacrifice. You give up the pleasures of the flesh to receive the gifts of spirit. The restricted diet, combined with the continued ingestion of powerful shamanic plants puts your body into an exceptionally clean chemical state that opens the door for new experiences by making you more receptive, perceptive, sensitive, aware, and conscious of many realities.

Awareness is the essence of what the work is all about.

During the diet, the subsurface of your psyche comes up, exposing fertile layers for ayahuasca to work in. When you drink the medicine in the circle under the supervision of the *ayahuasquero*, it assists you in entering into morphogenetic fields, meaning the energy fields of certain plants or animals, which the shamans call the mother of the plant or animal. The shaman leading the session opens the door to those fields to use the morphogenetic energy of jaguars, snakes, plants, birds, or other animals to secure help from them in healing, caring, transforming, and "seeing."

The analogy of the ancient tradition of the hunt applies to the diet. If one is hunting a jaguar, it is the same as hunting its morphogenetic field, making it inappropriate to engage in sex or eat certain oily or fragrant foods, because they generate strong human sexual or food odors in your body and soul, which the jaguar, in its highly aware state, will smell and avoid.

The diet involves avoiding anything that displeases or annoys power animals or teacher plants. To do so offends the spirit and mothers of the plants as well as the "owners of the forest," inviting retaliation, since these beings have the power to both inflict and remove illness. Ayahuasca shamanism is about relationships with the forest and how one lives in relation to the forest. Mankind's original way of looking at nature was to listen to it in silence and learn from it. This is the shamanic way.

Nature is the teacher.

FORTY-SEVEN

Immersion

The only word that comes to mind to describe waking up in the rain forest is *primeval*. The jungle is never quiet. The continuous buzzing, calls, and chatter of insects and animals fill the day and night, each with their own quality. The night is the loudest. You can find yourself awake in the total black of predawn and sense a subtle shift in the nature of the sounds around you. Though you can see nothing, you know by the shift that sunrise is approaching.

As the new day dawned through rising jungle mists, the noise of the jungle's night life drifted into the lower-energy buzz and hum of the day, punctuated by the cries of birds and animals that sounded sweeter, lighter, and less insistent than those of the night. What the life that fills the jungle day lacks compared to the volume of the night it makes up for with its visual orchestra. Bugs of all shapes and sizes buzzed and crawled everywhere, as did the lizards. Birds, smaller animals, and bigger ones seen less frequently moved on the ground and in the trees. Hummingbirds, butterflies, moths, and insects of all sizes, colors, and markings flitted in the sun, the most spectacular of them *el morpho*; a large, iridescent, cobalt blue butterfly that flutters up and down the waterways.

I had a slight headache but couldn't eat because of our first ayahuasca session that day. The shaman's helpers, a beautiful dark-haired young girl and a short, dark-haired, muscular young man brought me crushed, sweet-smelling huayusa leaves for my plant bath to pour on myself and let dry. I filled the bucket with water from the creek by my *tambo* and took my first plant bath, which I thought of as a baptism, my first direct contact with a jungle plant and my "initiation" into the plant diet.

I made my way down the trail a short while later and met the rest of our group at a circular, thatch-roofed dirt-floor open-air hut about forty feet in diameter called a *maloca*, perched high on a riverbank. Its size accommodated about twenty people sitting around its inner perimeter. José came and set up his altar of shamanic objects, consisting of pan pipes, flutes, and other musical instruments, quartz, other stones, items carved from wood, trinkets, charms, plants, rattles, Agua de Florida (a sweet flower-smelling perfume used by most Peruvian shamans), and a couple of containers of dark brown viscous ayahuasca.

Before our first and only daylight session, José chose the second healing plant that we would be working with from four additional helper plants. He chose a plant called bobinzana for me and about a third of the group. Bobinzana is a tree that grows by the water with roots that go deep into the earth and wide-reaching branches that grow high into the sky. Its purpose, like its form, is to ground you solidly into the earth, at the same time lifting you high into the spirit world above. Its description made me think of the *axis mundi*, the tree of life that connects heaven to the earth.

Our daylight session began with José doing his usual whispers, whistling, chants, and songs called *icaros* and *mariris* to open the circle and sing to the elemental spirits of the healing plants we planned to work with. After the opening, he poured our servings into a small silver shot-glass-sized cup, blessing each dose with a prayer before we went up one at a time to drink.

Because of ayahuasca's multidimensional, densely packed, nonverbal, symbolic way of communicating, words can never adequately express the content of the visions it brings, so I can only approximate the breadth and depth of what I experienced in those first rapid-fire, red-hued visions. Drinking ayahuasca in its natural environment made me feel connected to the earth while receiving an education on multiple levels of my being that surpassed anything I could read or imagine. As my geometric visions expanded and unfolded, I experienced more of the progression of consciously evolving life, finding myself in the primordial mud and slime among colonies of ants, spiders, and snakes.

I saw countless streams of ants crawling up and down vines, then the vines turned into snakes and serpents. I understood the meaning of the cosmic serpent and why mother ayahuasca chose to manifest in the form of a vine, and why snakes were so prevalent in ayahuasca visions. The vine and the snake are one and the same.

I soon found myself covered with ants and spiders. Then I became ants and spiders, eventually transforming into a smaller insect eaten by bigger ones. Masses of colorful snakes intertwined themselves everywhere, writhing into a huge mass until bigger ones started swallowing smaller ones. Then still bigger ones swallowed them until a giant one remained. Before I knew it, it swallowed me, dropping me into what I thought of as a cosmic luge, passing me through its body, digesting me into different realms and ways of being. I felt fear, but my awe and fascination outstripped all other emotion as I passed through a frenzied introduction into the myriad dance of nature firsthand.

Watching the bugs, then the snakes eating each other, I understood how everything consuming everything else is the process of life. I felt plunged into the heart of the earth, where I understood the endless cycles of life, death, and rebirth. My lesson here reinforced my conception of the progression and expansion of consciousness up through the increasingly complex and sophisticated layers of intelligence from one-celled animals to humans.

My visions started out dark at the roots where life ends in rot and begins anew. I saw how the plants and animals die and rot into the earth to supply the nutrients for the plants that grow out of them in order to feed everything else. I understood these cycles of life because I experienced them directly on multiple levels.

My visions went from the bottom up into the snakes, then up into the flowers, emerging from the bloom and the blossoms that reach up toward the light of the sky. My visions felt like they tied in with the bobinzana I would be working with because its roots go deep into the earth and its blooms go high into the sky, connected by the *axis mundi*, the tree of life.

We had a powerful circle that day, which turned out to be my sixth or seventh time doing ayahuasca, and I still hadn't shit or vomited. I began to believe myself blessed or special in some way, thinking I didn't need to purge. I didn't struggle against it. It just didn't happen. Prior to this circle, I had never taken a second dose, but when they asked, Geramy went up for one, so I figured after jumping into the wasp swarm with him, I might as well jump into this too, so following his example, I took a second dose.

José played more music until I became emotional and started crying when he played his guitar. Its indescribable beauty touched my heart while he sang to the spirits of the plants, to Pachamama, the spirit of Mother Earth, and Sacharuna, the spirit of the plants. While he played, massive, multicolored giant orchids bloomed and blossomed at high speed, coming at me as if from the side. These orchids seemed to harbor a higher intelligence beyond that of mere flowers, as if they embodied an otherworldly alien life form that had mobility. As our group dealt with the discomforts of sweating and vomiting, José explained that ayahuasca is about the body and that our bodies are our teachers. Breathing is important, as it can move you through difficult spaces you may find yourself navigating. In my visions I learned that humanity in the greed and ignorance of its materialistic consumer culture has been trying to force nature to conform to its imposed forms, but nature always comes back into balance, and when it does, we will see the growing consequences of our ignorance.

I connected more with the group after the session, especially with one of the ladies who participated. I found myself thinking specific thoughts, then hearing her voice them, and when I spoke some of my thoughts, she told me she had been thinking them at the same time.

I made my way back to my *tambo* late in the afternoon in fading daylight while still under the influence of the ayahuasca, feeling surrounded by magic and closer to the earth than I had ever felt before in my entire life. For dinner that night they brought a bowl of rice and one baked *plátano*. I would spend that night and all the next day and night alone before meeting with the group the following night for our second session.

As if to confirm my sense of magic, I had a strange experience that night in my hammock. While I was lying perfectly still, my hammock swayed back and forth in a wide arc, as if Mother Earth watched over me, rocking me like a baby. My *tambo* sat in a hollow and the air felt completely still. With no external motion, I kept my body perfectly immobile, yet the hammock rocked me for a long time with no movement on my part and no rational explanation for the force behind the rocking.

Later that night José and his helpers came with my first three doses of bobinzana, which they said to drink a couple of hours after I ate. They told me that it works on your insides and can be mildly visionary. José told me to take the second dose first thing in the morning after waking. After he left, the *mariri* he had been singing at our session softly repeated itself over and over again in my head, perhaps as a lullaby to the rocking I had received.

I drank the first bitter, smoky, charcoal-tasting dose of bobinzana at the appointed time, gulping it down as fast as possible to minimize its unpleasant taste, and felt its first subtle effects soon afterward. I sensed nothing visionary, only a slight shift in perception, more along the lines of a different sense of the awareness of my body.

The guard came by later that night and pointed out a spider with his flashlight, sitting at the center of a huge web that spanned the trail at face level, saying, "*araña.*" Its body looked to be about half the size of my fist. I made careful note of its location. The last thing I wanted was a face full of a Jurassic spider in the middle of a dark jungle night, especially under the influence of ayahuasca.

FORTY-EIGHT

Revelation

 awoke the following morning from a deep and dreamless sleep, something I would experience after each ayahuasca session. José stopped by to check on me, and his helpers came soon after with a bowl of boiled *quinoa* and another *plátano*. I didn't feel hungry like I expected, but I ate anyway, realizing that I felt very awake, uplifted, spiritual, and highly aware, as if the doors of my perception had been cleansed and my senses expanded.

I went out to look at the life surrounding my *tambo* with my newly discovered clarity and realized that many of the insects looked much like the plants they crawled on. I looked at what I thought of as a leaf and it moved, revealing itself as an insect. A beautiful moth landed on the ground and spread its wings, making it indistinguishable from the leaves it had landed in. I looked at a piece of wood and thought it a hummingbird. Then I saw a leaf by the creek and mistook it for a bird. What I initially missed I now saw as a magical world of subtle merging between animal and insect forms with those of the plants for the purposes of camouflage. I took this as evidence of the oneness and interconnectedness that pervades all.

Torrential rains came later that afternoon in a rising crescendo that swept through the forest, bringing with it rumbling thunder, lightning, and another piece to the puzzle of the cycle of life. The power of nature's cleansing force brought leaves and dead branches crashing down all over the place, making room for and providing nourishment for new life that would grow from the water and rot of the old and dead. When it stopped, the songs of frogs and crickets filled the air, bringing still another facet to the sights and sounds of the jungle.

Each time the jungle transitioned, whether from day to night, night to day, sun to rain, blowing winds, or the cessation of rain, the animals and insects responded with a distinct change in the nature of their orchestra, giving the impression that they sang and danced under the direction of the weather, who served as their conductor.

By the time my dinner of rice, a *plátano*, and a small, bony piece of chicken came that night, my energy had flagged, but the food gave me an instant lift. José also brought more bobinzana. I drank three glasses from the first pitcher. Now he instructed me to double the dosage; two before bed, two in the morning, and two in the afternoon before tomorrow night's session.

I couldn't wait for the second session, which would be my first in the jungle at night. I expected ayahuasca to take me on an orderly learning progression by continuing my experience along the path of consciousness and evolving life forms the way I already had, from the ground up, through the bugs, culminating in the peak experience of being swallowed by the snakes. I hoped my second session would take me all the way up to the jaguar. I wanted to experience what it felt like to be swallowed by a jaguar and possibly become one, but I would soon learn that ayahuasca has an unpredictable agenda and a unique intelligence all its own.

After downing my last two glasses of bobinzana, I crawled into my platform bed, which soon felt as if it swayed to the point that I thought it would fall over. I grabbed onto it hard and found it solid. Then I realized that it wasn't the bed swaying.

It was me.

Unlike the magic rocking hammock that had really swayed on its own, this time I swayed internally. My equilibrium was off, due no doubt to the increased intake of bobinzana. I eventually drifted off to sleep until I awoke in the middle of a cool, damp night to the songs of frogs and crickets. I felt ravenously hungry. I crawled out of bed and looked up at the moon, visible through the shifting jungle mists that rose languidly from the ground. Mild panic danced beneath my hunger, but I steeled myself and in the midst of my inner battle I saw myself as a warrior who was becoming more of a warrior every day. I realized that a true warrior is a warrior with himself, which is exactly what I was doing there by myself in the jungle on the diet. I had to conquer my body with my mind. I remembered José telling us that our bodies are our teachers and that working with ayahuasca is about mastering the body.

My revelation continued unfolding with the understanding of my body as a holographic reflection of the earth, which is an entity itself. My body is of the earth, from the earth, and would return to the earth in death the way I saw the plants, bugs, and animals doing here, to become food for new repeating cycles of life. My task was to master my body and my self. I could have panicked when bugs and snakes swallowed me in my visions and the alien orchids had rushed into me, but I held my composure and mastered my fear, accepting whatever came.

I contemplated my lifelong fascination with fear, thinking about how I had jumped into the wasp attack to help Geramy. Then I remembered a forgotten memory of a Fourth of July when I was sixteen. Big Jim had carelessly lit a bottle rocket and knocked it over into a pile of rockets beside the bottle, igniting them. Rockets went off, flying everywhere, and my ten-year-old little sister stood screaming in the middle of it. All I could think about was one of the rockets hitting her in the eye, so I ran and pushed her to the ground, shielding her with my body, taking a number of stinging rockets in the back. This memory heightened my awareness that my body could feel and experience fear and hunger directly, but my mind could overcome it. The silly frights I experienced with the bugs and the frog in the darkness reinforced this lesson. In the end it did come down to mind over matter.

I thought again of my desire to hunt the jaguar in my visions and thought of myself as a warrior who hunts the darkness. Whether I saw it in the jungle or the landscapes of my visions, the truth was that the darkness ultimately lived inside of me. Ayahuasca had the ability to find and exploit my deepest fears, bringing terror in direct proportion to the depth of the particular fear it tapped into, constituting part of an amazing process of self-discovery. Realizing that I still had much of the night to pass, I crawled back into bed and soon fell into a deep sleep that carried me into one of the most profound, mind-boggling, transformative experiences of my entire life.

While sleeping I drifted through a dream of parking underground at some kind of event that brought me to a hotel room where I found myself in bed with an unidentified woman whom I loved. An indistinct shadowy male presence reclined on the other side of her. I felt deeply connected to this woman but also a little put off by the other male presence, so I rose from the bed.

My "love" became more defined as a strikingly beautiful, dark-haired young woman who said, "Come with me. We're going to go celebrate and be happy." I started leaving the woman and the male presence, wishing with all my heart that they wouldn't kiss or have any sexual contact.

I awoke briefly and climbed out of my bed, compelled to look up at the moon. Then I went back to bed and drifted off to sleep, picking up where I had left off, walking and hugging "the woman of my dreams," who had shifted her identity to a woman named Patty whom I had a romantic interest in. Both of us felt excited that we were going to be married. We stepped into an elevator and saw an older woman there. I dropped a briefcase I had, apologizing to the older woman. She smiled and all of us felt happy.

We went to an office and I saw some of the guys who worked for me. They were concerned that I was not where I was supposed to be at work, so I became concerned and ran around the back of a building until I found myself behind a house, my mind full of excuses for why I hadn't been where I was expected.

I recognized the house as that of my friend Teresa's, where I had attended a number of parties. Then I became lucid and realized that I was still asleep in the jungle in Peru and had eight more days before I had to go back to work, yet the dream world felt more than real. I looked over and saw a hand cart that I had knocked over. Then I saw people coming to Teresa's house to attend a party.

Now that I had become fully lucid, I could take over the dream, fly, or do whatever I wanted, but I didn't want to startle the people coming to the dream party by flying in front of them and messing up their party by scaring them and making them aware that I was in a dreaming body.

A group of young girls came, so I picked up a broom and clowned around, marching along the back of the house like a soldier in an effort to fit in and stay lucid to see what would unfold if I remained lucid without taking control of the dream. While this scene unfolded, I remained cognizant of being in two places at the same time, fully aware of my physical body sleeping in the jungle while my conscious awareness inhabited my dream body. What boggled my mind beyond all imagination was the fact that *the world of the dream had a far greater immediacy and a greater reality than the known physical reality of my sleeping body.*

I went into the house and saw a big stained-glass piece of art hanging in the doorway, depicting a Mayan-like god. I remembered that in my "real life" I had spent some time exploring Mayan ruins with my friend Teresa, so seeing this piece of art confirmed my conviction of being in her house.

I went up some stairs to a couch, where I found my dream girl, this time in the form of a strikingly beautiful young blonde. I sat beside her on the couch and saw her once again in the company of the indistinct shadowy male presence, who appeared big, feeling this time like a friendly uncle figure.

He asked me for a hug, so I reached behind him and gave him a big, hearty hug. Then my dream girl said, "Hey, I want a hug too."

Overjoyed, I said, "Hell yes. You especially get one!"

I embraced her face to face with a strong, wonderful, loving hug. Then she gave me the most exquisite kiss I have ever received. Words fall short in trying to describe the sensation, so I can only approximate it, saying that in that wonderfully cosmic moment, her kiss infused me with instantaneous love, compassion, power, wisdom, understanding, and knowledge all rolled into one timeless yet transitory moment.

I awoke startled, suddenly back in the jungle, shaken to my core, feeling a deep loss, as if I had literally fallen back to the earth from a greater hyper-reality that had more depth and breadth than anything I had ever imagined or experienced—a reality that felt far more real than I felt even then, startled wide awake, back in my physical body.

FORTY-NINE

Rapture

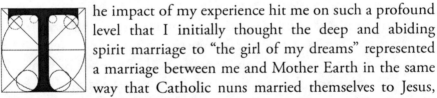he impact of my experience hit me on such a profound level that I initially thought the deep and abiding spirit marriage to "the girl of my dreams" represented a marriage between me and Mother Earth in the same way that Catholic nuns married themselves to Jesus, except in my case I had no illusions about celibacy. I felt this way because I sensed that every one of the beautiful young girls and the older woman that had shifted form in my dream were in fact one and the same woman who had the ability to change her form at will. Beneath all of her manifestations, I felt acutely aware of the same beautiful, loving feminine spirit that obliterated the boundaries of my wildest imaginings.

Memories of my dream girl and the emptiness I felt at losing her filled most of my waking moments that day. I replayed the dream and relived my cosmic kiss over and over, savoring every exquisite moment.

José told me that the dreams came because the bobinzana had started working with the other plants and the diet. When I went to the circle that night and we checked in with each other, I told everyone about my dream. Geramy called it a power dream and someone reaffirmed that becoming lucid and remain lucid in the dream without taking control had been the best thing to do.

We started our second session in the clamor and darkness of the jungle night. José began by honoring the spirits of the forest and the teacher plants with his prayers, songs, and whispers. I took a full dose, letting José fill the cup to the brim. He looked closely at me, his eyes saying, "Are you sure you want this much?"

I did, and soon felt the physical effects of the ayahuasca washing over me, at first seeing visions of spiders. When José played his charango, I saw flowers and butterflies. Then, without warning, I beheld the sweet, beautiful girl of my dreams revealing herself to me in my visions in the most exquisite way imaginable. I resisted her initial urgings, but she gently persisted until I let her in and embraced her. When I did, Santa Teresa De Avila spoke in my mind in what I can only describe as telepathy, yet her communication encompassed far more. I felt her presence inside of me as an integral, intimate part of me as our spirits joined as one. As she informed me of who she was, her words or thoughts all came to me in Spanish, and to my further awe and amazement, *I understood every word she said.*

All of the pieces that had been hints from my dream coalesced in my mind, making total sense. She had come to me in the first short dream. Then I awoke to look up at the moon, another symbol of feminine energy. When I went back to sleep, she came to me again, picking up in the new dream right where she had left off in the first one, leading me to the gradual revelation of her presence. Now she merged with me here in all her glory. Not only did she merge; she possessed me, and in that sublime and ecstatic rapture, I possessed her with equal fervor, embracing the sweet essence of her femininity with an undying love. No matter how much of myself I gave away, I couldn't seem to give enough of myself to equal her love. Never before had I felt such an overpowering love entwine and become such an intimate part of me. Teresa's loving presence overwhelmed and rocked me on all levels, profoundly merging our spirits to the core of my being. Physically, the love felt so deep, intimate, and all encompassing that it felt erotic to the point of embarrassment. I felt so united with her in every cell of my being that I could not hide how I felt.

After an interminable moment of rising discomfort at my eroticism, she reassured me that there was nothing wrong with my feelings. They were the natural physical manifestation and the genuine expression of my deepest love, and to feel shame for the biological expression of a love so pure and powerful was nothing to be ashamed about and certainly nothing to hide and suppress. It was in fact cause for celebration.

For quite some time, my legs and my body twitched, rocked, and convulsed like an epileptic, only this felt like pure bliss, and in the throes of my ecstasy I understood and experienced firsthand the true meaning of rapture, and I never wanted it to end. In the midst of my experience, I came to terms with my sense of connecting and feeling married to Mother Earth in my dream, realizing that Santa Teresa was an aspect of the cosmic mother, the feminine side of the One. I understood this conceptually and wordlessly on all levels.

When the session ended, I asked everybody I knew who Santa Teresa De Avila was because I had never heard of her prior to this night. Someone told me they remembered a church named after her. Someone else told me she had been a famous Spanish Christian mystic, which totally blew me away because I had rejected Christianity wholesale and had come to the jungle expecting to embrace a full-on pagan experience like being swallowed by a jaguar.

I later discovered that, like me, Santa Teresa had rebelled against the organized church and is considered the patron saint of visionaries, mystics, and epileptics, but not in the sense of the medical condition of epilepsy; more in the sense of people who twitch and convulse in their visions the way I had. Santa Teresa is also the second most widely read author in Spain, second to Cervantes, who wrote the adventures of Marco Polo. She died in 1582 and had been a close friend of Saint John of the Cross, the author of *The Dark Night of the Soul*. There are numerous stories of her spontaneously levitating, among them a particularly poignant one of her doing so while holding John's hands through the window of her cloister. After she died, her body didn't decompose. Like the bodies of other saints, it continuously gave off the sweet scent of flowers.

I felt unworthy of her loving attentions and could not for the life of me figure out how such a lowly, anti-Christian, one-time career criminal, and certified dirty white boy from Dorchester could even come close to being anywhere near deserving of the gifts of love and spirit she blessed me with. I went back to my *tambo* that night feeling exceptionally light and blessed, and when I finally fell asleep, I slept deep and dreamless, waking up feeling a sense of loss and disappointment that she hadn't come to me more in my dreams. I hoped and hoped that she would come back to me and have longed for her blessing and the sweet blissful gift of the touch of her spirit ever since. Though I felt a tangible loss now that I was no longer in her presence, I was convinced that somehow Santa Teresa De Avila represented the key that comprised the piece to a puzzle that would bring everything together for me.

FIFTY

The Language of the Heart

On the night prior to the next session, I dreamed of being caught in the middle of a gang of violent, ugly, threatening bikers who brandished big knives that they cut their hands open with to try to intimidate me. This dream stood in sharp contrast to the bliss and beauty of my Santa Teresa dream, and it was not lucid or hyper-real in any way. These angry menaces wanted me to be their spokesman who would make their voices heard. I didn't realize it then, but I figured out later that these rowdy, violent, and unruly male aspects of my shadow came from my Dorchester roots, and the aware self in the dream played the role of mediator between that extreme polarity that existed inside of me between this testosterone-fueled gang that I had identified with all of my life and the sweet, wonderful femininity that recently touched my heart. I knew that one day these wildly disparate and opposing energies would merge and eventually balance themselves out inside of me.

I had a final dream of being in a poker game with other people in my life, and in it I saw coins everywhere. Though none of these dreams became lucid, I hoped they might lead to another vision along the lines of the one I'd had of Santa Teresa, so I went into the third session expecting a continuation of the theme of Christian mysticism, but true to its unpredictability, ayahuasca brought me something totally different and unexpected.

We were well into the plant diet by our third session and really "cooking," as they liked to say, so we didn't need as much ayahuasca. I drank about three quarters of the dose I'd had previously, and to my mild disappointment, I didn't fall into rapture with the spirits of any saints or mystics. I now understood that ayahuasca is the essence and voice of Mother Earth, who opens your heart so you can explore it, and in this mid-session I found myself plumbing the depths of my heart. I received many revelations about those I loved, and I was warned about dark forces that impinged on my life, posing possible dangers.

I hoped for an undeniable connection between my dreams and visions the way I had with Santa Teresa, and in her own strange, fickle way, Mother Ayahuasca obliged. One of my warnings was about someone I considered to be a dark force in the lives of some I cared about. While I was pondering this, one of the speakers in the circle addressed it as if reading my mind when they started talking about how to deal with your enemies. The gist of the lesson stated that you can never truly defeat your adversary. They will never go away, so the only way to defeat them is to make them your ally. This is especially true when you look at yourself in terms of being a divided self. Acceptance is the only way you can reintegrate such disparate, obnoxious, and unhappy aspects of yourself.

To my surprise, even my dream about playing poker held meaning when the speaker talked about the medieval origin of the now standard deck of playing cards and how they represented the quest of the seeker during the crusades. The four parts of the sacred quest represented the four pilgrimages. The first pilgrimage went to Spain, the home of Santa Teresa, only it went to the town of Santiago de Compostela, known in English as Saint James the Apostle. This symbolized the way of the sword, and what you received from the way of the sword was power. In the original decks they depicted this as a sword. In the modern decks it is represented by spades.

Next came a pilgrimage to Jerusalem to find the route to the Holy Grail. When you found the Holy Grail you gained the ability to see and perform miracles. This quest became symbolized by cups in the old decks and diamonds in the modern one.

The next went to Rome, represented by clubs. When you completed this pilgrimage, you gained the ability to contact, communicate, and travel in other worlds. This had the form of a wooden club held like the sword in the old deck. In modern decks it takes the form of the clover-like "club."

The final pilgrimage stood for the occult path to the mystery, which went to the hidden place, the route to the heart. The final destination and purpose of the journey was to find the gold, originally represented by gold coins. No one knew the route to this. You had to find it yourself. This destination lies within your heart, within yourself. Obviously modern decks have the original heart.

These spoken revelations dovetailed with what I had dreamed, adding to the depth of my dreams' impact and meaning. What struck me about my dream of the card game, the coins, the final destination and last lesson of the crusader's pilgrimage, and the nature and teachings of ayahuasca were the words of Carlos Castaneda: "A warrior must follow a path with heart." It made sense on multiple levels, and there in the jungle doing the diet, dreams, and visions, and in my life in general, I did follow a path with heart and spirit rewarded me.

In the final parts of the session, I traveled far into the spirit world, reaching out to my sister, her kids, and others in my life I loved and cared about, touching their spirits with mine, which I felt had been freed from my body to travel beyond the normal limits of time and space. After that night's session, I went back to my *tambo* and once more slept deep and dreamlessly, waking up the next morning feeling weak and lightheaded. I made a couple of small trips from my *tambo* but didn't go far and quickly ran out of what little energy I had, so I spent most of the day sleeping, doing my best to recharge myself with whatever energy I could. Later that night I had a vivid dream wherein I attended a party full of people with lots of colorful costumes in a big house with many different rooms. I had a sense that I knew everyone there. The party goers looked like sprites, pixies, elves, and other creatures, and the costumes ranged from bizarre one-eyed monsters to butterflies, insects, and other beings. It felt like a Mad Hatter's ball. They taunted and teased me in a playful way, then they took me to a room with a drum set that had huge leaves for cymbals. Charlie Watts, the drummer for the Rolling Stones, played them. I wanted to play, thinking that I could do a better job, but I couldn't bring myself to do it. I sensed an overriding sense of expectation from everyone waiting for me to do my part, whatever that was. I awoke pondering the dream, feeling slight puzzlement along with the sense of expectation the many beings in the dream left me with, hoping that in its own strange way, ayahuasca would provide the missing pieces that would make sense of it all.

Feeling physically weak but highly aware and more open than I'd ever felt in my life, I went to the fourth session that night. I left early to give myself plenty of time to make it to the *maloca* as I grew dizzy every few steps and had to stop frequently when I felt faint. By the time I reached the *maloca*, I felt fragile and vulnerable like an infant, but in spirit I felt strong. Because of my heightened sensitivity, I drank a little less of the brew and still had an intense and powerful experience.

FIFTY-ONE

The Journey into the Heart within the Heart

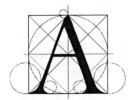 heavy rainfall came with the onset of our visions, complete with bright, startling flashes of lightning and explosive bursts of thunder. As the rains came, José told us a story of doing a healing session on a barge in the middle of a river. In the place where he worked, the clear water allowed him to see all the way to the bottom. In his visions it came to him that the water went back up into the sky and then rained down again, forming into the river, and that the evaporation and condensation process was the earth breathing. With this realization he found himself back in the womb in a blissful and oceanic place.

As our session unfolded, José not only worked with the whole group, but he also did individual healings for each one of us. In my case he played a beautiful melody on pan pipes and sang a healing song. When he did healings on others, he looked at me while I drummed, silently encouraging me to drum along with his songs to reinforce the healings. I felt honored that he included me and played my part with a steady beat. In the times I drifted, he looked to me, encouraging me with his eyes to stay with him and keep the beat, which I did.

As if responding to our intentions and José's actions, a drama unfolded like a scene out of a fantastic magical movie where the lightning and thunder worked in concert with José, who looked like a wizard in his ceremonial robes. During particularly difficult healings, he gestured dramatically, stomping his feet and waving his arms in concert with each thunder burst. It looked and felt like their power followed his bidding, adding to the impact of his healings.

After our healings, José told us about Quechua words and their meanings that related to different parts of the body. While speaking he told us of his struggle to sort out their meanings between English, Spanish, and Quechua in the context of a session he had held with fifteen psychiatrists who came to him for help. He found it amusing that fifteen degreed professionals had come to see him in the jungle; a man who by all definitions of the word was illiterate. In his efforts to tell them the process he was taking them through, he became confused between the three languages, and in a classic Freudian slip, what came out of his mouth was "Your head is up your ass."

He didn't mean this and hadn't been thinking it, but it came out that way. He tried to retract what he had said, then realized he had spoken the truth and started to laugh. The more he tried to correct himself, the harder he laughed. He could hardly get the words out while telling the story because he laughed so hard in the telling. His laughter made us all laugh, making it still harder for him to get his words out, which made us laugh even harder. I laughed so hard that I became breathless until the force of my laughter took me out of the circle and out of the jungle completely, transporting me into a world of multicolored geometrical dimensions of patterns and colors far removed from the present time and place. Never before in my life had my laughter transported me so far into worlds so abstract and so alien. I felt astonished that I even returned.

During this session I had many personal revelations and ecstatically beautiful visions, all relating to the nature of spirit, how it manifested, and how it guided me. I was also shown directions to take with my life, things I needed to do, and confirmations of other things I had learned. I felt inundated by how much I learned and the amount of information I took in during that one session.

In the same way that my other dreams came to fruition and made sense in my ayahuasca visions, so did my Mad Hatter costume party dream. With what I can only describe as an inarguable sense of knowing, ayahuasca completed my dream puzzle by showing me that all the familiar dream beings who expected me to "do something" were more divided aspects of myself, much like the bikers, only these aspects represented more benevolent and playful parts. The deeper meanings of these two dreams tied in with our session and were driven home in a most exquisite way when I heard a story in the last part of the night that made it all make sense in a way that only ayahuasca could.

I was told that tickets were bought for a performance in a magical theater. In our minds we went into the theater and took our seats in the front row to watch a play called *Life*. The lights went down, the curtain rose, and the play began. In the play I watched the events, incidents, battles, and moments of ecstasy that constituted my life, including the time spent there in the jungle. The play continued unfolding until at some point I began to think that I could do a better job than what I saw being performed in the same way I saw Charlie Watts on the drums in my dream, thinking I could do a better job if I got up to play. With this impulse I rose from my seat and went up on the stage to act myself, putting on different costumes and playing different roles. Some of them fit and others didn't.

I found myself split in two, both watching the play and acting in it. This went on for a while until the acting became stale, so I shifted and became the writer of the play as it happened, changing lines and actors, which gave me a great sense of power. Then I found myself split into three, watching myself, acting, and writing as I went along until I remembered that I wrote the play for money, for a producer. More time passed until I grew bored and decided to become the producer, splitting me into four people—watcher, actor, writer, and producer—until I gradually remembered that I had produced the play for someone else who was an invisible shadow. Then I remembered that part of this invisible person happened to be me, splitting me into six people.

In that sense I became the play in the same way I did in my life and in my dreams, being both the dreamer and the dream. In my life and in my dreams I continue playing my part in creation, entertaining and projecting myself by continuing to write, act, produce, and watch. As the play drew to a close, the curtain came down and I left the theater, walking out with the distinct feeling that I had just witnessed a great truth, but I wasn't quite sure exactly what that truth was.

When the session wound down, I felt exhausted but spiritually charged and elated from the personal revelations and ecstatic visions I had received in our session. I made my way back to my *tambo* in the darkness of the jungle and dropped into another deep and dreamless slumber. I awoke the following morning, thinking that in my spiritual quest I had come deep into the Amazon jungle to the heart of the earth and in coming to the heart of the earth I had journeyed deep into the center of my own heart.

My outer and inner journey became one and the same hologram.

FIFTY-TWO

Answered Prayers

I drank the last of my bobinzana the following day and drifted in and out of the edges of sleep all day, at one point seeing the hazy vision of an old woman coming to me and thinking of her as the spirit of bobinzana. We broke the fast that night with a pinch of salt, which symbolized the doorway back from the other world, and then we feasted on a community meal of chicken soup with vegetables, pasta, and rice; without a doubt the absolute best chicken soup I ever ate. The idea of breaking the fast with the salt as a doorway began the process of gradually re-assimilating ourselves back into the "normal" world.

Back at my *tambo*, I realized that the food had strengthened me and that the whole experience would soon come to an end and my dreams wouldn't have the same otherworldly quality they had taken on. I understood that my intellect struggled to put my dreams into linear meaning while my dreams had their own illogical continuity that tied one thing to the next. In reality my dreams held densely loaded meaning in the form of holographic symbols. The essence of shamanic thinking is a symbolism that contains denser meaning beyond what linear thought can embrace. As Western "rational" thinkers, we stay busy trying to impose our own meaning upon the world, which is limiting and close-minded by nature of its own linearity.

How can we ever hope to comprehend the vast mystery of life on earth and in the cosmos with such a narrow perspective?

With these thoughts in mind, I drifted off to sleep, awakening to heavy rain with broken fragments of dreams drifting through my mind. In my dreams I had watched a movie, then I was in the movie, then I was directing and writing the movie, just like in the story of the play called *Life* I had heard in our last session. I found the experience both educational and amusing.

We made our way through the pouring rain that morning and gathered for breakfast, feasting on papaya, watermelon, bread, and oatmeal with raisins and fruit, and spent the morning talking until the rain let up and we could get back to our *tambos* without getting soaked. When the rain stopped later in the afternoon, José took us on a tour of the area, showing us a variety of healing plants and their uses. After the tour we had a short time to rest before our final ayahuasca session that night.

The final session turned out to be incredibly intense, and I found myself a little irritable and on edge before going into it because of my highly sensitized state. José opened the circle with his prayers, songs, and chants, and as if by magic, soon afterward everything I thought and everything I felt gelled in a wordless way into solid meaning and comprehension.

When José sang and played his music, it touched me to such depths that I traveled through endless dimensions of colorful patterns and emotions. Each musical note made my body quiver and twitch in ecstasy, as if I were epileptic. At one point my body swayed, snakelike, with a sublime, independent life of its own. I found out later that Santa Teresa had the same physical responses while in rapturous visionary states. As is always the case with ayahuasca, words are inadequate in trying to describe the intense experiences you have, so I can only say that in this final jungle session everything I had learned during my ten-day *dieta* became summed up in a way that gave me a sense of completion. All I had learned and experienced in my ten days of dreams and visions made sense in its own nonsensical way, and I had much to share. A number of people told me that I had come to the jungle not only for myself but for many others. After this final session, I understood what they meant.

Exhausted, satisfied, and still under the influence of the brew, I made my way back to my *tambo* for a few hours of sleep before a six-in-the-morning wake-up call that would have us loading up the canoes and heading back down the river to the life and world that awaited us after we had been isolated from it for close to two weeks.

While I was crossing the creek in pitch dark about fifty yards from my *tambo*, my flashlight winked out and wouldn't light again. I steeled myself as panic and frustration careened through me and tried cautiously stepping forward, slipping on the rocks and running water at my feet in the darkness. I stumbled, wondering how I could find my way to my *tambo* in such total darkness, all the time worrying about walking into the huge spider's web that I knew waited for me somewhere along the path at face level. As I moved through blackness, I prayed and berated myself for not paying more attention and being more prepared.

Ahead, off to my left, where I sensed the edge of the creek's bank in a space of about a fifty-foot ellipse, a mass of fireflies clustered in a surreal gathering, providing otherworldly light in an otherwise pitch-dark jungle. I paused and admired their beauty in spite of my fear. Then I continued stumbling through the water, trying to temper my frustration with reason, finally finding the creek bank. I thought I had made good progress onto it when it felt like the earth dropped out from under my feet and I fell down a steep embankment, tweaking my knee. I sat in the water for a moment feeling helplessly lost, trying to figure out what to do.

Remaining immobile in the water wouldn't get me anywhere, so I rose slowly, crawling up the embankment, once more moving inch by inch along the ground on trembling legs, walking into trees until I literally walked into my *tambo*, banging my head on one of its posts. I stood for a moment, giving thanks while taking stock of myself, covered with mud that had seeped into my shoes and socks. My whole body was wet, sweaty, and stinking. Playing it back in my mind, I understood that the jungle taught me an incredible lesson that I am forever thankful for.

I had resolved to give myself a drink of water for my parched throat and to use the rest of its precious, refreshing coolness to bless myself and give thanks to the mother for such a profound lesson and for getting me back to my *tambo* safely. With this in mind, I stripped off my clothes, made an offering and a prayer, and poured the cool clear water over my head, all the while thanking Mother Earth for her blessing of water and life.

At that precise instant, in an answer to my prayer, I heard the rising crescendo from a wall of rainfall that came sweeping across the jungle, rushing toward me, blessing me in its downpour as Mother Earth drew in a deep breath, surrounding me with her promise of love and life.

FIFTY-THREE

Validation

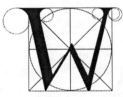e arose at six the following morning and took the canoes back down river to the village we had set out from and ate a breakfast of chicken and rice before piling into a line of beat-up cars. After another two-hour wild ride down dusty, muddy, pothole-filled roads, we reentered the two-stroke stink and clamor of the bigger jungle town, checked into our hotel, showered, changed, and went out to eat.

As soon as I had a free moment, I found a telephone to call my mom and let her know I was all right. I didn't want to freak her out in my babbling excitement, but I couldn't contain myself, and before I knew it I found myself telling her about my visions and rapture with Santa Teresa De Avila. She remained quiet and I sensed something tangible on the other end of the phone line. Then I thought, *Now I've done it. I told her way too much and she thinks I've really gone off the deep*

end. If she wasn't worried about me before, she's scared out of her wits for me now.

Finally I said, "Ma, what's wrong? Was it something I said?"

She hesitated, then said, "You're the first person I ever told this to in my entire life. As you know, your grandmother raised us Catholic. I was never a big believer in the church, but I have always believed in God. Growing up as a little girl, she assigned each of us saints to pray to, and every time I have ever prayed in my life I have always prayed to my saint, Saint Teresa of Avila."

Epilogue

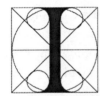f I ever had any doubts about the reality of my jungle experiences, my conversation with my mother proved to me deep in the recesses of my heart that spirit *does* matter. In my inner journeys, I have discovered that I am a warrior with my many selves who has hunted the darkness where the lost and forgotten aspects of my self have raged in fear and hopelessness. Fear and death have been my greatest teachers, but it is the spirits of the plants who have shown me the many faces of Mother Earth, Father Sky, and the oneness that binds them all to the infinite cosmos that lies beyond this narrow and fragile dream we call reality.

My story is a myth, a word whose original meaning meant "One's truest and deepest story," and it is in this spirit that I have laid my life before you to show the many paths I have walked in search of truth, meaning, and my endless fascination with the boundaries, real or imagined, that blur, define, or redefine what each of us thinks of as real.

We all have our personal truths that we carry in our hearts through the agony and ecstasy of each transitory moment of our existence that transforms who we are from moment to fluid moment. These inner truths made manifest in our conscience are proof of a greater reality made painfully evident in the fear and helplessness that grip us in the face of our own inevitable deaths.

My path has taken me from early, lost innocence in a civilized "jungle" to the real jungle, where spirit did indeed touch my soul and show me the infinite teaching of the limitless expanse of consciousness that *spirit* truly *is*.

My inner and outer sojourn from splintered dissonance has led me toward an evolving wholeness that is itself evolving toward an even greater oneness encompassed by All That Is so that my divided and chaotic selves can continue transforming from a dark chrysalis of selfishness into a magical butterfly of selflessness that will wing its way homeward, back to the One.

My explorations into inner worlds have shown me that we are far more than we ever imagined. In them spirit has revealed to me that I am star dust, manifest in the wind, the rain, the rivers, the lakes, and the oceans. I am the rocks and the mountains and the ground that gives life. I am the grasses in the fields, the flowers, trees, vines, bushes, funguses, mosses, and molds. I am all of the creatures of the earth:— my brothers and sisters who fly, walk, crawl, slither, and swim—for I am a keeper of the cosmic fire that burns within every one of them. I am in all of the plants and all of the animals because I come from the heavens, but I am of the earth. I am all of these things and all of these things are within me because I am a child of the stars, born of the earth. Though I come from spirit, I will never forget that I am my mother's child, and I would not have come into this magical place we call the earth were it not for the union of my mother and father.

The gift of their complementary wounds polarized me, forcing me to rise above the paradox of anger and sorrow to a transcendent, emotionally balanced perspective. It is truly a miracle that I survived the darkness and difficulties that I faced in my early life. SomeOne loves me. SomeOne has been watching over me, guiding me, and protecting me each step of the way, and as it turns out, I wasn't unloved and abandoned after all. I got lost. Now my shadow and I are finding our way home.

BIBLIOGRAPHY

Davis, Wade. 1998. Shadows in the Sun. Washington, D.C.: Island Press

Eliade, Mircea. 1964. Shamanism: Archaic Techniques of Ecstasy. New York.: Pantheon Books

McKenna, Terence. 1992. Food of the Gods. New York.: Bantam Books

Oeric, O. N., and O.T. Oss. 1976. Psilocybin: Magic Mushroom Grower's Guide: A Handbook for Psilocybin Enthusiasts. Quick American Publishing

Shulgin, Alexander, and Ann Shulgin. 1991. Pihkal: A Chemical Love Story. Berkeley.: Transform Press

_____ 1997. Tihkal: The Continuation. Berkeley.: Transform Press